READ THIS BOOK
OR YOU'RE
GROUNDED!

A SECRET GUIDE TO SURVIVING AT HOME

Wayne Rice

READ THIS BOOK OR YOU'RE GROUNDED!

A SECRET GUIDE TO SURVIVING AT HOME

Wayne Rice

Read This Book or You're Grounded: A Secret Guide to Surviving at Home

Copyright © 2003 by Youth Specialties

Youth Specialties Books, 300 S. Pierce Street., El Cajon, CA 92020, are published by
Zondervan, 5300 Patterson Ave. S.E., Grand Rapids, MI 49530

Library of Congress Cataloging-in-Publication Data

Rice, Wayne.
  Read this book or you're grounded: a secret guide to surviving home /
by Wayne Rice.
      p ; cm.
Summary: A Scripture-based, common-sense approach to understanding
parents and making them happy for Christian or non-Christian teens who
want more freedom and respect.
  ISBN 0-310-25049-8 (softcover)
  1. Parent and teenager--Juvenile literature. 2. Parent and
teenager--Religious aspects--Christianity. 3. Teenagers--Family
relationships--Juvenile literature. 4. Teenagers--Conduct of
life--Juvenile literature. 5. Parents--Juvenile literature. [1. Parent
and teenager. 2. Christian life. 3. Conduct of life. 4. Teenagers.] I.
Title.
  HQ799.15 .R53 2003
  306.874--dc21
                                          2002011795

Unless otherwise indicted, all Scripture quotations are taken from the Holy Bible: New
International Version (North American Edition). Copyright © 1973, 1978, 1984 by
International Bible Society. Used by permission of Zondervan.

Web site addresses listed in this book were current at the time of publication. Please
contact Youth Specialties via e-mail (YS@YouthSpecialties.com) to report URLs that are
no longer operational and replacement URLs if available.

Edited by Rick Marschall
Proofreading by Lorna M. Hartman
Cover and interior design by Mark Rayburn Design
Illustrations by Matt Lorentz
Production Assistance by Nicole Davis

Printed in the United States of America

04 05 06 07 08 09 / DC / 10 9 8 7 6 5 4 3 2

- Listen Up
- Take Time to Hang with Them
- Learn to Forgive
- Stay Plugged In
- Remember the Law of the Farm

- My Parents Aren't Around Very Much
- My Parents Don't Care What I Do
- My Parents Split Up
- My Parents Try to Communicate Through Me
- My Stepparent Is a Pain to Get Along With
- My Parents Are Always in a Bad Mood
- My Parents Expect Me to Be Something I'm Not
- My Parents Are Too Strict
- My Parents Push God on Me Too Much
- My Parents Are Not Christians, but I Am
- My Parents Are Immigrants from a Different Culture
- My Parents Are Bad Examples for Me
- My Parents Are Abusive
- My Parents Don't Listen To Me
- My Parents Are Not My Real Parents
- My Parents Are Cheap
- I Can't Tell My Parents What I've Done
- My Parents Don't Want Me To Leave Home
- My Parents Think They Know Everything
- My Parents Embarrass Me

For my three kids
Nathan, Amber, and Corey
with gratitude

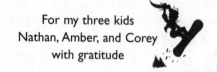

"**Y**ou expect me to read a book about understanding parents? Come on; give me a break! If anybody should be reading a book, it's them!

"No, it's not like I hate them or anything. They aren't such bad parents. I know they probably love me, and I know that they're doing what they think is best for me. It's just that I'm tired of being treated like a child.

"I know I'm young and make mistakes, but they make mistakes too. I have a brain, and I've done a lot of things right that they never give me any credit for. I don't need them telling me what to do all the time. I don't need all their stupid rules!

"You don't know what it's like! When I'm at home alone, I'm happy. I don't do anything wrong, at least nothing real bad. I just mind my own business. But then they come home, and everything changes. All of a sudden I hate being home. It's like being in prison. I'd run away, but where would I go?

"What I really want is to move out and get my own apartment. I know I could survive without their help. They'd be surprised, but I could do it. I'd get a job or maybe stay in school. I don't know what I'd do for sure, but at least it would be my decision, not theirs. I'd show them, and I would be so happy!"

Meanwhile—back in the real world—you're stuck at home, forced to live with parents who are always getting in your face, driving you absolutely nuts, infringing on your inalienable right to life, liberty, and the pursuit of all the cool things that you absolutely have to do to survive as a normal, well-adjusted teenager.

Kind of depressing, isn't it?

Think moving out is the best solution? Well, one of these days your parents will be happy to arrange that for you. Just be patient. It won't be long before you'll have all the freedom you want and more. But right now, you've got to deal with parents.

Want a better relationship with them? Tired of all the hassles? Want to be happy now instead of later? Well, you can be.

You can change things at home. You can turn all those lose-lose battles into win-wins if you want to. It's all up to you. You can have more freedom, a better quality of life, and parents who think you're wonderful if you take time to read this book, give it some thought, and put it into practice. Or, don't read the book and stay grounded. The choice is yours.

Here's the deal. If you want your parents to trust you more, give you more respect, and not treat you like a box of rocks, you're in luck. All you have to do is figure out how to make *them* happy—and this book will help you do just that. I'll tell you how to get along with your parents without giving up your fun or your coolness. It's really not all that complicated or difficult. Once you learn how to meet *their* needs, you'll not only start getting what you want, but the relationship you have with your parents will improve big-time. One thing's for sure. You aren't going to get what you want by rebelling and treating your parents as if they're the enemy. Despite what you've heard, they're not. Nobody loves you more than your parents do. They are just, well, parents. And parents take a little explaining.

So start reading!

EYES IN THE BACK OF

(MYTHS
ABOUT
PARENTS
YOU'RE
BETTER OFF
FORGETTING)

THEIR HEADS

I spend a lot of my time talking to parents. In fact, I travel to cities across America almost every week trying to explain YOU to them. I do this in a seminar called *Understanding Your Teenager*. Hey, don't laugh. I actually do it for a living!

I often start the seminar by debunking myths about teenagers. One of them is called *The Myth of the Teenage Werewolf*. This myth, simply stated, is the belief that all teenagers go bad. No kidding. Some people think that when kids become teenagers—unless they're locked in their bedrooms and given

Here's an idea: Ask your parents to pull out their high school yearbooks, then ask them to sit down and explain why they thought those goofy looking hairdos and ridiculous clothes looked so cool. Or, next time you see grandma, ask her what your mom or dad did to give her all that gray hair. You'll probably come to the frightening realization that your parents remind you a lot of you.

massive doses of Ritalin—they automatically turn into uncontrollable, rebellious monsters who wreak havoc on society, destroy families, and ruin their lives forever.

Sound like you? I didn't think so.

But a lot of people believe this myth. Why? Maybe they believe it because that's all they hear. So much media coverage about teenagers shows juvenile delinquency, school violence, teens on drugs, teen gangs, teens and sex, teens driving under the influence, teen suicide, and every other kind of teen problem. People start to believe that's how all teens behave. Never mind that the vast majority of teenagers stay out of serious trouble or that most of the bad stuff going on in the world involves adults, not kids. When people are constantly bombarded with bad news about teens, they sometimes paint all of you with the same stereotypical brush.

But here's the real problem. If your parents buy into the *Myth of the Teenage Werewolf*, they'll probably treat you and your friends as if it were true. They'll trust you less, give you less freedom, and worry about you a lot more than they need to.

Not fair, is it? But that's what myths and stereotypes do. They make life tough for the group being stereotyped. It's hard enough to be a teenager without everybody automatically assuming you're going to be a major problem. That just makes you want to live down to everybody's expectations. But you don't really want to do that.

Well, a few myths about parents need to be debunked too. You know all teenagers are not alike. Well, neither are all parents, and you shouldn't lump them all together as if they were. Parents get a lot of bad publicity around the school lunch table and in the popular media. If you buy into that, you'll mess up the relationship you and your folks have even more. Let's start by getting rid of some of that "myth-information" about parents as much as possible. Only then will your situation at home improve.

– – – – – –"PARENTS ARE YOUR ENEMY"

We may as well begin with the queen mother of myths about parents. While parents (also known as *homo sapiens painus in neckus*) can sometimes make life difficult, they are not your enemy by a long shot. If your parents are on the attack, think of it as friendly fire.

Yes, they do attack. They threaten, criticize, humiliate, nag, accuse, interrogate, and punish. They lob scud missiles like, *"When are you going to start acting your age?"* or *"Can't you do anything right?"* These questions may cause you to retaliate with a few dumb bombs of your own like, *"You can't make me!"* or *"Get out of my life!"* And then it's Desert Storm all over again. Your house becomes a battleground.

But that still doesn't make your parents the enemy. Trust me on this one. Later, I'll explain why your parents get on your case so much, but for now, keep in mind that conflict is not that unusual between teenagers and parents (duh). That's because you are growing up and seeking more independence and freedom, and that scares your parents. They worry because they know they are losing control of you. They don't always know how to react to this, and quite frankly, neither do you. So you engage them in a few skirmishes. But that's why I've written this book—to help you learn some survival strategies to deal with parents who are sometimes their *own* worst enemies.

As you get older, you'll realize your parents are not enemies, but allies. They love you more than anyone else on earth. The strange thing is that sometimes the people who love each other the most get on each other's nerves the most. Think about it. If someone you don't know criticizes you, you don't really care, but if a family member or close friend does, it really hurts.

Remember, most of the hassles you're experiencing at home right now are temporary. When you finally move out and start living on your own, you'll probably have a great relationship with your parents. Most people do.

But what you want is a better relationship with your parents right now. After all, your relationship with your parents is probably the longest, deepest, and most meaningful one you'll ever have with anybody. Your parents brought you into the world. They cared for you when you couldn't care for yourself. They gave up a lot for you when you couldn't give anything back. Someday you'll want to be close to them. Maybe you don't feel that way now, and that's okay. Just know that they're not your enemy. They're on your side, and if you look hard enough, more often than not you'll find them cheering you on no matter what you do.

"PARENTS ARE CLUELESS" – – – – – – –

If you believe this myth, you've been watching way too much TV. Helpful hint: The Simpsons are only cartoon characters, and most of those other TV families exist only in scriptwriters' warped minds. Right now it may be popular to portray parents as bumbling idiots who have to be rescued by their clever, resourceful, and extremely bright children—but come on, give your parents a break! They may not be rocket scientists, but they probably know all they need to know to do a good job of raising you.

On top of that, they have a whole lot more life experience than you do. I guarantee they've learned a few things about life that you might want to learn yourself someday if you'll only pay attention.

Of course, you may believe you're a more highly developed life form than your technology-challenged parents. How could they possibly understand the complexities of the universe when they can't even tell a CD-ROM from a DVD?

Okay, so they grew up in the dark ages. But keep in mind that it was your parents' generation (and even some before theirs) that came up with all the cool gadgets and gizmos that make your life so advanced and interesting today. One of these days, your kids will benefit from *your* brilliance, all the while thinking you're about as intelligent as a stump.

Don't underestimate your parents' intelligence. Clueless as they may seem about the anatomy of a PS2 or X-Box, they'll get a lot smarter in a few years. A wise man once said, "At 16, I couldn't believe how ignorant my parents were. But at 21, I couldn't believe how much they had learned in only five years."

- - - "PARENTS DON'T UNDERSTAND YOU"

Actually, your parents probably understand you better than anyone. Who has the credentials to understand you better than your mom or dad? Who's spent more time with you than your parents? Who knows your life and family history better than your parents? If your parents don't understand you, then nobody does!

"But my parents don't remember what it was like to be a teenager. They've been adults so long, they have no idea what I'm going

through."

That may be true. But your parents *were* teenagers, and they do remember what it was like to be one. Their memory is just selective. They remember (1) the highlights and (2) the lowlights—the really good stuff and the really, uh, bad stuff (which they never tell you about.) They could remember a lot more, but they're too busy trying to be the age they are right now to spend a lot of time living in the past.

That's why they sometimes act like they don't remember anything at all. Or they say dumb things like *"When I was your age I had to walk twenty miles to school everyday...in the snow...with no shoes...uphill...both ways...fighting off dinosaurs..."*

If you really believe your parents have no idea what it's like to be a teenager, take the initiative to enlighten them. Tell them what's going on in *your* life, and before long, they'll be experts!

"PARENTS DON'T WANT YOU TO HAVE ANY FUN" - - - - - - - - - - - -

Yeah, right. They want you to be miserable—just like they were when they were teenagers. You've heard all their stories. They spent their entire teen years cleaning their bedrooms, doing homework by candlelight, listening to "good" music, milking cows, plowing fields, helping old ladies across the street, reading the Bible, et cetera, et cetera.

> **My parents are too strict. They are always scared I'm going to get hurt.**
> —Heather, age 13

Speaking of the Bible, the "parents don't want me to have any fun" myth probably got its start back in the Old Testament when the first teenager in history (whose name was Cain) thought he'd take his brother Abel out for a little fun in the backyard (see Genesis 4:8). And that is the last we hear of dear little brother Abel.

Here's the problem. You want to have fun, but your parents want you to be safe. Sometimes those two wants are in direct conflict with each other. Parents aren't against fun so much as they're against having you be the lead story on the evening news. They know from experience that some fun can be dangerous, illegal, unhealthy, or all three. Every time they hear or read about some kid who gets killed in a car crash on the way home from a party where alcohol was served, they imagine you in that car. That's why they sometimes act as if they don't want you to have any fun. They really don't want you dead.

There's nothing wrong with having fun, but it's possible to have fun without making your parents worry half to death. Maybe you think safe fun is boring and very uncool. But wait until you have kids of your own (if you live that long). You won't want them to get their kicks playing in the freeway either. If your idea of fun is putting yourself or others in danger, your parents are right to stop you from doing that. That's how they prove they really love you.

Have all the fun you can have. Even the Bible encourages you to do that (check out Ecclesiastes 11:9). But for heaven's sake (and yours, too) make sure it's the kind that will pass muster with Mom and Dad. Go out of your way to let them know exactly what you'll be doing. Make a big deal out of just how safe and sensible it is! Give them details about where you'll be, who'll be there, what precautions have been taken, and when you'll be home. The more information you give them, the better. If you'll communicate with your folks and help them get what *they* want (no worries), then you'll get what *you* want (lots of fun!)

– – – – – – – "PARENTS ARE SLAVE DRIVERS"

So your parents treat you like an indentured servant? They force you to toil your life away doing the stupid chores and boring jobs *they* don't want to do? Well, unless you live on a farm at the turn of the century (not this century—the *LAST* one), it is highly unlikely this myth is true. Not too many parents out there really produce children just to have a cheap labor force to plow the fields, milk the cows, harvest the crops, or even take out the trash. Parents no longer view their offspring as hired hands or

expect them to earn their keep by cleaning the garage or trim-
ming the rose bushes.

*"But my parents do. Why else would they constantly be on my
case about doing chores, being lazy, thinking money grows on trees, getting a job, not contributing to the family, blah, blah, blah. Why can't they
just leave me alone?"*

Well, if they did, they wouldn't be very good parents. Really,
they don't care about how much money you can earn for them,
or how much time you can save them, or how clean your bedroom can possibly get. What they care about is *you*. See, they
keep having this recurring nightmare starring you at age 35 living
on welfare, eating a steady diet of government cheese, and living
in a van down by the river. After a few bad dreams like that, you
can understand why they get real concerned about your appar-
ent inability to pick your socks up off the bathroom floor.

Look, I know it's extremely inconvenient and very uncool to
have to do actual work when you could be having fun, but parents have the right to ask you to chip in and help out once in a
while. Some economists figured out that the average American
parent spends close to a quarter of a million dollars per child by
the time their kids graduate from high school. And unless you're
the next Britney Spears or Justin Timberlake, you probably aren't
going to contribute much to that. So why not be willing to contribute some of your time, energy, and talent to make your parents' lives a little easier? They'll not only be a lot more generous
with you now, but they'll start dreaming about the day when
you're a successful entrepreneur who helps pay for their retirement home in the Bahamas!

"PARENTS DON'T WANT YOU TO HAVE FRIENDS" – – – – – – – – –

Just because your parents don't want you to hang out with the new
kid down the street who was just released from prison, looks like
a human pincushion, has neon hair, and a portrait of Osama Bin
Laden tattooed on his chest, and creatively works the f-word into
every sentence, doesn't mean they don't want you to have any

friends.

Okay, I exaggerate a little. He doesn't actually have neon hair. But the fact remains—your parents aren't against you having friends. They know friends are important to

> *I absolutely hate it when my parents argue with me in front of my friends.*
> —Jenna, age 13

you. After all, friends are important to them, too. They know that friends are good, not bad, and they probably *want* you to have a lot of friends. They just don't want you to have friends who might influence you to do things that are unhealthy, unsafe, or immoral. They remember all too well some pretty bad friends they had as teenagers, and they fear you'll do the same. They believe if they can protect you from bad people, they can protect you from bad behaviors.

But parents don't always do their homework. Chances are they don't know your friends too well. They often make wrong assumptions about your friends, especially when you don't offer much information about the company you keep. They suspect the worst and react as if they don't want you to have any friends at all.

You have control over this situation. After all, you choose your own friends. Your parents can't choose them for you.

So, step one is to choose your friends wisely. Nobody's perfect, of course, but you're probably a pretty good judge of character. What you want to do is avoid relationships that will be a hard sell to your parents. Like it or not, their fears are well grounded. Even the Bible teaches, "bad company corrupts good character (1 Corinthians 15:33)." You can't really argue with that. It's up to you to choose friends who won't drag you down.

Next, introduce your friends to your parents. I know this sounds terrible because you don't want your parents to embarrass you or your friends. But don't keep your friends a big mystery. Invite them over, and let your parents get to know them. Your parents will be much more likely to let you spend more time with friends they've met and know something about.

Here's something else to think about. Parents can sometimes be a little bit *jealous* of your friends. You see, when you were little, *they* were the most important people in your life. You crawled up in your mom or dad's lap and gave them hugs and kisses. They had all kinds of time to be with you.

But now that's all changing. You treat them as if you're allergic to them. When they walk into the room, you leave. Parents naturally take this personally and feel rejected and alone. Think about it. If a close friend suddenly decides she doesn't want to be with you anymore, it hurts. If someone else (instead of you) becomes your friend's friend, you may feel jealous or angry with that person. You don't even know them, but you don't like them because they stole a relationship that used to be yours.

That's why it's a good idea to spend plenty of time with your parents even though you want to spend more time with your friends. Your parents will feel less threatened and less angry that someone they don't know is taking you away from them. They'll be a lot friendlier to your friends.

"PARENTS CONTROL YOUR LIFE" - - -

Your parents may *wish* they could control your life, but they gave up on this one a long time ago. Really. All parents can control is themselves...and maybe their stuff—their car keys, their checkbook, and their house. But they can't control you. Unless you're locked in your bedroom 24/7 with an armed guard stationed outside your door, nobody controls your life but you. Every day you make the decisions that determine what you do and how you respond to the world around you. No one else can make these decisions.

Does that mean you have control over everything? Of course not. Nobody has control over *everything* except God. And in case you haven't noticed—you are not God, nor is your mom or dad. None of us controls the world or what happens in the world, but we do control how we respond to the world and what it throws at us.

I know, you don't like all those stupid rules. But stupid rules are part of life and making them is part of a parent's job description. Parents get to make the rules because that's their job and because they care about you. At least give them credit for that. And while you don't control the rules they make, you do control how you respond to them. Your parents don't have control over that.

Teenagers who just don't want to accept responsibility for their lives usually believe the "parents control my life" myth. They'd rather blame their parents for their screw-ups. They enjoy feeling like victims, like losers. But that's their choice. They'll get what they want—they'll be losers for the rest of their lives. But you don't have to make that choice. You have total control over your attitude and your behavior. You are in the driver's seat.

What kind of life do you want, anyway? Whatever it is, it's not up to your parents to provide it for you. The story of your life has to be written by you. Set some goals and go after them, starting today. Your parents may try to limit what you do right now, but that's a life challenge you'll face long after you leave home.

> *My mom told me "If you
> have a problem, come talk to me." Well I
> did that, and she just got mad. I want my parents
> to let me learn from my mistakes, but so far all
> I've learned is that you don't want
> to tell your parents anything.*
> —Annysa, age 15

"PARENTS WILL USE WHATEVER YOU TELL THEM AGAINST YOU" - - - - -

"Mom, Dad...I have something I want to tell you."

"That's wonderful. We're so pleased that you want to share what's going on in your life with us, dear. But first, we need to tell you something. (1) You have the right to remain silent. (2) You have the right to an attorney. (3) Anything you say can and will be used against you in order to take away your privileges, put you on restriction, alienate your friends, and in general, make your life miserable. Now...what was it you wanted to tell us?"

Makes you want to open right up and spill your guts, doesn't it?

Fortunately, you won't hear anything like that from your parents or anybody else's. Still, the myth that parents can't be trusted with information is one of the most popular and most damaging. Some kids never talk to their parents because of it. Or if they do, they do it *very carefully.*

"But my parents can't handle the truth."

Baloney. What that usually means is *"If I tell my parents the truth, I'm toast."* See, it's not your parents who have a hard time with the truth. More often than not, it's *you.* When you say "I'm being honest with my parents" when you really means "I'm confessing something I've done", you can't blame parents for not handling it the way you think they should.

Maybe you just need some advice. Who do you turn to? Where do you go when you have a problem you can't solve or an important decision to make? Most teenagers say they talk to their friends first. Maybe a counselor or youth pastor. But rarely parents! Does this make sense to you?

Believe it or not, your parents are almost always in the best position to help you with problems or give you the guidance you need. They love you, they care about you, they know you, they want to protect you, and they want what's best for you. That doesn't mean they'll always keep secrets the way you think your friends will. (Actually—and I hate to be the one to tell you this—you don't have that many friends who wouldn't turn snitch if they thought they had something to gain from it. So wake up and smell the Starbucks.®) Unless your parents are the rare exceptions, they're always going to be in the best position to take whatever information you give them and use it wisely, in your own best interests. They, of all people, are on your side.

> *There's no respect, no trust, no communication. They won't let me grow up. We're always fighting. Nothing is ever good enough. Everything can always be better. I tried to talk to them and work things out, and they just say my problems are all in my head.*
>
> —Nicole, age 18

So don't buy into the notion that parents are just waiting for you to give them information they can use to ruin your life and spoil your fun. If you do, you won't need parents to ruin your life. You'll do that on your own.

"PARENTS DON'T WANT YOU TO GROW UP"

Some kids believe this myth because their parents keep treating them like children. *"I guess they just don't want me to grow up!"*

Get real. Do you really think your parents want you to stay a kid so they can keep nagging you forever about getting your homework done? Do you think they want you to stay home taking up valuable space they could easily turn into a sewing room, office, or day spa? Do you think they really want to continue shelling out bucketloads of money it takes to keep you in food, clothing, insurance, transportation, education, recreation, and all the other stuff you require?

Well, think again. Maybe a few (and I mean *very* few) professional parents out there just can't stand the thought of watching their children grow up, but so what? Parents have nothing to do with whether or not you grow up anyway. How fast you grow up is totally up to you. They can't make you take some kind of growth-stopping pill that keeps you sucking your thumb for the rest of your life. If and when you do grow up, your parents will simply have to deal with it.

The growth we're referring to here is more than just

physical, of course. Obviously you'll go through puberty (if you haven't already), which will make you get bigger, stronger, and grow hair in strange places. But that doesn't mean you're an adult in your parents' eyes. You can be seven feet tall and lift a steam locomotive over your head, and parents will still treat you like a child as long as you continue to *act* like one. Age and physical size mean nothing to the parents who have to constantly pick up after you, help you with your homework, get you where you need to be, remind you several times a day to do your

chores, force you to eat healthy food,
and so on. The longer you act child-
ish, the longer they will keep
the baby stroller parked right
outside your bedroom door.

If your parents are any-
thing close to nor-
mal, they get
down on their
knees and pray
every day

that   you'll
grow up into a
well-adjusted,
self-reliant adult. They can't wait to see you make more than one
responsible decision in a row and give them a glimmer of hope
that you can make it on your own. It's a no-brainer. If you want
your parents to *treat* you more like an adult and less like a child,
all you have to do is *act* more like an adult and less like a child.

— — — — — — — —"PARENTS WON'T CHANGE"

When do you think they got stuck? How old were they when
they decided to set themselves in concrete and become the
Neanderthals they are today? Just because they still listen to the
Doobie Brothers and they're a bit slow to understand why you
absolutely *must* have your tongue pierced, doesn't necessarily
mean they can't or won't change.

Parents change like everybody else does. In fact, they *want*
to change. They certainly don't want to be parents forever. As
wonderful a son or daughter as you may be, they no doubt look
forward with great anticipation to the day when you grow up, out
and into a life of your own. After a few tear-filled goodbyes,
they'll high-five each other, downsize their budget, turn your bed-

room into a walk-in closet, and stop worrying about being such a bad example for you. They'll change all right, and so will you. One of these days you'll look at your high school yearbook and hardly recognize the goofy-looking kid pictured above your name.

But what about right now? You're frustrated because your parents won't budge. They keep giving you the same stupid answer when you ask if you can stay out all night with your friends. They go ballistic every time you bring home lousy grades on your report card. They keep lecturing you about doing chores and picking up after yourself and being home on time for dinner. They never change!

But what do you expect? They're your parents. If you're waiting for them to change into people who *don't* care what you do or where you go or who you're with, you'll probably wait a long time.

And in case you're wondering, you can't change your parents, so don't even try. You may think you can wear them down by arguing, whining, or giving them as much grief as possible, figuring they'll finally give up and give in. But that approach backfires, even if it temporarily gets you what you want. Angry and exhausted parents don't give their kids more respect or more privileges; they give less. You'll get change, all right, but probably not the kind you had in mind.

So what can you do? I have good news for you. *You may not be able to change your parents, but you can change you.* And the funny thing is—when *you* change, your parents will change right along with you. If you want to know how to do this right now, jump ahead to chapter four.

But here's a sneak preview. Want them to stop treating you like a child? Stop acting like one. Want them to give you more freedom? Start being more responsible. Want them to stop nagging you about the condition of your room? You know what to do. Really, the ball's in your court. If you want your parents to grow up, you gotta grow up first.

PARENTS ARE PEOPLE TOO

(FACTS ABOUT PARENTS YOU'LL WANT TO REMEMBER)

Okay, now that we've debunked some of the more popular myths about parents, let's get to the facts, Jack. This chapter contains the absolute, uncensored truth about parents. Your mom and dad wanted to tell you all this stuff someday, but since they haven't gotten around to it, I will. Just think, you'll be the envy of all your friends when you go to school and explain their parents to them. They'll be amazed at how much they didn't know. Quite frankly, I didn't know much about parents either until I became one.

Why do you need to know about parents? Because the more you understand about parents, the easier it is to live with them. As the Bible says, "Understanding is a fountain of life to those who have it, but folly [myths] brings punishment to fools" (Proverbs 16:22). Most wars result from misunderstandings and clashes between very different cultures. While you and your parents have a lot in common and know each other pretty well, all kinds of things need some explanation.

Here's a quick disclaimer. These facts are generalizations. They may or may not apply to every single parent in the world. But there's a better than even chance that these generalizations do apply to yours.

PARENTS ARE ABSOLUTELY NECESSARY - - - - - - - - -

Come on; admit it. You need your parents. Nobody makes it into this world without parents. Parents are just about the biggest fact of life there is. This may come as a shock, but without parents, you don't exist. As they say in biology class, "If your parents didn't have any kids, don't plan on having any yourself." And here's a really disgusting thought. Take your age and add nine months to it. That's about how long ago it was when your mom and dad got all romantic and made…um…you! After you stop groaning (or throwing up), thank your lucky stars they did.

What if your parents aren't your biological parents? Big deal. You still need them. Whether you have foster parents, adopted parents, or were found in a cabbage patch, you still can't survive without a parent or two. Your mom and dad—whoever they are—play a huge role your life, whether or not they provided the sperm and egg that resulted in the person with your particular DNA. Parents have a much bigger purpose than just making babies.

Here's the deal. God created us to be raised by parents. There's no other way. I think we can safely say that no one in the history of the world has made it successfully into adulthood without at least one parent to love them, provide for them, teach them, discipline them, and keep them from walking out in front of a bus. If you think it's tough living with your parents, try living without them. On second thought, don't.

Your family is a very special thing. It may not be perfect, but it was still ordained by God. In Genesis 2:18, God said, "It is not good for the man to be alone," and so he invented families. And unlike the animal world, he made human families to last a lifetime. You'll never stop being part of your family, and your family will never stop being part of you. That's why many people trace their families back for generations. Families tell us a lot about who we are.

Interestingly enough, God liked the idea of families so muc, he decided to become part of one himself. That's what Christmas is all about. In the first chapter of the New Testament, Jesus is introduced to us with a description of his family tree. He had a mom (Mary) and a stepdad (Joseph), and the Bible says he was obedient to both of them. Think about that. The King of Kings and Lord of Lords put himself under the authority of two inexperienced parents. It's no wonder he grew up to be such a fine young man (Luke 2:52). It couldn't have happened any other way.

Be thankful for your parents. I know it's trendy nowadays to put down families and blame everything that's wrong with the world on parents, but don't buy into any of that nonsense. Your parents are good for you, a gift from God, and you need them more than you realize. Learn to get along with them, and you'll learn to get along with anybody. They are your ticket to a successful and happy life.

PARENTS HAVE A TON OF RESPONSIBILITY – – – – – – – – – –

You think you've got responsibilities? Try being a parent.

Seriously. When you get married and have kids of your own, whether you're ready or not, you'll find yourself suddenly strapped with a ton of responsibility. Besides all the time and expense that goes into raising children, you'll find yourself stuck with the daunting task of making sure your little angels don't self-destruct before they reach the age of accountability. Parents discover right away that children are hell-bent for destruction beginning the day they come home from the hospital. They won't eat their Gerber, but they'll swallow marbles, snails, silver polish, roach pellets, cleaning fluid, or any other dangerous substance they can put into their mouths. They'll ignore the perfectly safe toys Santa brought and play with razor blades, ice-picks, electric wires, or balcony ledges if they exist anywhere within reach. It's no wonder parents get into the habit of yelling the word *no* as frequently and loudly as possible. *No* is how they save their children's lives.

> *My dad doesn't have a life. His life is his work. He's never around, but I'm used to it now.*
>
> —Ashley, age 15

Apparently your folks did a pretty good job. You're still with us. Maybe it's time to thank your parents for at least getting you this far. Of course now you'd like for them to back off, stop being so responsible, and just leave you alone. You can probably take it from here, right?

Perhaps. But unless you live somewhere in the world that doesn't have an area code, your parents probably remain legally, financially, and morally responsible for you until you move out on your own or reach the age of 18, whichever comes first. Even though they can't control your behavior (only you can do that), they still feel obligated to provide you with food, shelter, clothing, education, health care, and all those other amenities of life that you probably take for granted. No wonder they find it necessary to interrogate you constantly and keep their rules in place. Since they are responsible for you, they believe they have the right to know what you do, where you go, who you're with, and what risks are involved. Can you blame them?

If you think your parents are too strict or too demanding right now, be patient. As you get older, your parents will gradually give you more free-dom and pass a lot of that responsibility to you. Try not to blow it. Show them that you can handle it, and you'll probably

get a whole lot more. Your parents just need some assurance that their little tax deduction can make good choices and wise decisions, and they'll be more than happy to cut the apron strings forever. Meanwhile, count your blessings. It won't be long before you'll have nobody to blame but yourself.

PARENTS HAVE FEELINGS JUST LIKE YOU DO

Ever have a bad day when you just wake up on the wrong side of the bed? You really don't want to talk to anybody, and you certainly don't want anybody to make any demands of you. Maybe you have a good reason to feel lousy, but you can't really explain why you feel the way you do. All you want to do is just listen to music and chill, but your parents start nagging and scolding, getting on your case about being lazy or having a bad attitude, and before you know it you go ballistic. Pretty soon everybody's yelling, doors are slamming, and now on top of the bad mood you were already in, you're feeling hurt, angry, and misunderstood.

Thank goodness, bad feelings don't last forever. We survive them. But as we all know, feelings like these can make us do and say things we really don't mean to do or say. When emotions get out of control, a vicious cycle of bad feelings can cause *everybody* to behave badly, including your parents.

You may think that because you're a teenager, you have some kind of special permission to be emotionally volatile (after all, isn't that how everybody *defines* adolescence?). But what about parents? Aren't they supposed to be in control of their emotions at all times?

Well, that's another myth you can toss into the old porcelain fixture. Your parents have feelings just like you do. They may have more experience at hiding them or handling them, but they feel them just the same.

Let's take a peek inside a parent's head for a moment. Most parents like to think of themselves as generous, loving people who do more for you than anyone. After all, they got up in the middle of the night to feed you, change your diapers, and rock you to sleep. They sacrificed their personal ambitions and worked long hours to provide a good home for you. From their perspective, they think they're entitled to a little obedience, appreciation, and respect from you. When they don't get it, they take it personally. They feel hurt, unappreciated, angry, and defensive. They start nagging and scolding, which of course makes you feel hurt, unappreciated, angry, and defensive, and the vicious cycle of bad feelings and bad behavior is off to the races.

When this happens, somebody needs to break the cycle. It could be them, but it may as well be you. A real sign of maturity is learning how to put yourself in someone else's shoes and try to understand what the other person feels. You always have a choice. You can throw fuel on the fire, or you can do something to cool things down. It's never easy, but you can do certain things. I'll give you some good ideas later in this book.

Meanwhile, the next time your parents are upset or angry or depressed or totally unreasonable, take a deep breath, try to give them some space, avoid saying or doing anything you'll regret later, and don't take things too personally. They may just be having a bad day.

PARENTS MAKE A LOT OF MISTAKES

Okay, I know this doesn't come as any big surprise, but it's worth mentioning anyway. It's also worth remembering next time your parents don't do the right thing or say the right thing or can't even figure out what the right thing is. Sometimes they blow it. They make mistakes. After all, they don't really know what they're doing. Professional parents just don't exist. Parents are on-the-job learners, and they frequently make mistakes. They probably won't admit this to you, but it's true.

When you were born, you didn't come with an instruction manual. Sure, parenting books can help (your folks probably have a few of them), but not one of them contains information on how to parent *you*. That's because before you were born, no one like you ever existed on the face of the earth. God created you with your own blend of personality traits, gifts, talents, abilities, and special needs that nobody else ever had. And as every retired parent knows, what works with one child doesn't always work with another. So whether you were your parents' first child or their fifteenth, they still had to figure out how to parent *you*.

> *They tell me everything they did wrong, so I'd know what to stay away from.*
> —Gretchen, age 12

And you know what? They're still at it. That's because as you get older, you continue to change. Every day your parents have to figure out how to be good parents for you based on who you are and who you're becoming. Some teenagers require more discipline and control, and others require less. Some need more love and attention while others need less. There's no science to this—it has to be done by trial and error. That's why parents sometimes make mistakes.

I know I made my share of mistakes as a parent. I said *no* to my kids when I should have said *yes*. I said *yes* when I should have said *no*. I didn't listen to them when I should have, and I didn't talk to them when I should have. Sometimes I was too strict. Other times I was too lenient. The problem with being a parent is you really don't know what you're doing until after you've done it. Even then, it takes a few years to realize what you did wrong or did right.

Don't hold your parents to a standard of perfection you can't even keep yourself. They do the best they can. You should realize that you have a lot to do with how successful your parents are. You can help them not make so many mistakes. If you can make life easier for them, there's a pretty good chance life will be easier for you. As I said earlier, parents generally learn how to parent from their kids. Parents with problem kids seem to be problem parents. Parents with good kids seem to be good parents. See, you have a lot more power to impact your family than you may realize.

Parents aren't perfect, of course. They won't always do the right thing. Your parents may disappoint you from time to time, and you'll wonder why they can't be more consistent, more reasonable, more trustworthy, or more like the parents of somebody else you know. But parent envy only makes things worse. Your parents are human, and they're probably the only parents you'll ever get. In their own inept way, they're doing the best they can. They need your understanding, forgiveness, cooperation, and love—in spite of all their mistakes.

PARENTS ARE NOT ALL ALIKE - - - - -

In the weird line of work I'm in, I get to speak to thousands of parents every year. So far, I don't think I've found any two that are alike. I'm always amazed at who God gives a license to be parents of teenagers these days. Some are young, some are old, some are tall, and some are short. Some are trim, some are overweight, some are in wheelchairs, and some are in jogging shorts. Some are married, some are divorced, some are brilliant, and some are a taco short of a combination plate. Some hang on my every word, and some act like they want to hang me. Obviously parents of teenagers do have *some* things in common, but mostly they're different. I can tell you this—of all the parents I've met in my lifetime, I still haven't met any like yours. Your parents are definitely unique.

But you knew that already. Your parents are probably so unique you think they belong in the circus. *"Ladeeez and gentlemen, step right up and see for yourself, the only parents in the world who won't let their daughter date until the age of 75! Believe it or not!"*

Here's the point…actually three points. First, don't believe all the nonsense you hear about parents from friends at school, TV and movies, popular music, and so on. Don't lump your parents together with all the bad examples of neurotic or abusive parents you hear about as if they were all the same. They're not, and you really can't have a good relationship with a stereotype. So drop the typical parent label, and cut your folks a little slack.

Second, don't be embarrassed because your parents are a little different. Okay, so they're a lot different. Still, you shouldn't concern yourself too much with what other people think. So what if they dress funny or talk funny or don't have an education or come from a different culture. Are they parents who love you? Do you love them? Don't be jealous of other kids who seem to have showcase parents. They'd probably like to trade their parents in for new ones too. Be proud of the parents God gave you, and celebrate their uniqueness.

Third, don't expect your parents to change in ways they can't possibly change. For better or worse, your parents were born with unique personalities, capabilities, talents, likes, dislikes, and special needs just like you. And most of their circumstances and the choices they made earlier in life are ancient history now and can't be undone. Maybe you wish your parents were smarter or funnier or richer or better looking, but you might as well wish for a spot on the local Quidditch team. Your mom or dad can change *some* things, but they can't change everything. So give them a break. Your family is a special blend of unique people who simply need to find a way to live in harmony. If you want that to happen, thank God for your parents, and try to understand and accept their strengths, weaknesses, and needs. They may just do the same for you.

PARENTS GREW UP IN A DIFFERENT WORLD – – – – – – – –

Do You remember when...
...cars didn't come with seat belts?
...homework was done on a typewriter?
...and without the aid of a spell-checker?
...airports didn't have metal detectors?
...neither did high schools?
...telephones had dials?
...TVs had antennas?
...and no remote controls?
...prime time meant family hour?
...drinking water was free?
...spam was food, not junk e-mail?
...smoking was allowed everywhere?
...gay meant happy, not homosexual?
...thongs were worn on your feet?
...all the girls wanted to look like Farrah Fawcett?
...everybody rode 10-speed bikes?
...Pac Man was the hot video game?
...Jordache was the hot designer label?
...the Rolling Stones were young?

If you don't remember the things listed above, ask your parents. I'm sure they do. The world they grew up in was way different from yours. The reason your parents sound so dumb saying "When I was your age…" is because in some ways they were never your age. When they were teenagers, they didn't have friends who thought it was cool to get a tattoo. They didn't know anyone with blue hair (unless it was grandma). They never visited an Internet chat room. They didn't worry about terrorism. DJs on the radio didn't use profanity. Designer drugs like ecstasy, GHB, and special K didn't exist.

> *I know my parents were my age once, but it has been so long ago that they don't know today's issues.*
> —Jessica, age 13

Again, that doesn't necessarily mean your parents don't know squat (see chapter one). All it means is your parents grew up differently. They have a difficult time understanding why you prefer pants that are too big for you or music that doesn't have a tune or jewelry that's invisible until you stick out your tongue.

Don't be upset with them if they find it hard to understand your world. After all, you probably find it hard to understand theirs. But people who care about each other take time to try to understand each other better. Talk to your parents about your world. Find out about theirs. Ask them to tell you about their teen years. Ask them to get out their yearbooks and photo albums and explain those goofy hairdos and weird clothes. You may be surprised to discover that your parents were young once, had dates, and probably steamed up a few car windows in their day (try to listen to this without throwing up).

PARENTS HAVE EXPERIENCE YOU DON'T

Here's a little math problem for you. Subtract your age from the average age of your parents (add your mom and dad's ages, then divide by two). Got it? Okay, the correct answer should be (drum roll, please)—the average number of years your folks have been around longer than you. It also should be the average amount of *experience* (in years) they have in their favor over you. They grew up in a different culture, but they didn't grow up on a different planet. Most of what they experienced growing up isn't all that different from what you're experiencing right now. They may seem a little old-fashioned at times, but when it comes to stuff like school, grades, friends, bullies, nerds, zits, popularity, dating, and yes, even parents, they have unquestionably *been there, done that.*

> *I try not to argue with my parents because most of the time, they're right.*
> —Taylor, age 12

So what? So, you actually can learn a lot from your parents. You can even learn from their screw-ups. Maybe you've heard the story of the farmer and his son who were walking across a field. The father says, "Son, if I step in a pile of cow manure, that's life. But if you watch me step in a pile of cow manure and then step in it too, that's stupid." Your folks may have some cow manure on their shoes, but there's no reason you need to make the same dumb mistakes they did.

The Bible puts it this way: "A wise son heeds his father's instruction" (Proverbs 13:1). God didn't say that because parents have more intelligence than their kids; they just have more experience. So wise up, and pay attention. Parents don't have to know everything to know more than you. Tap into their experience. Ask for their advice. They'll probably give it to you even if you don't ask, but ask anyway. They'll feel really important, and you'll avoid stepping in something.

PARENTS WORRY CONSTANTLY - - - - -

No kidding. Mostly they worry about you. Don't take it personally. It started when you were born. No...I take that back. It started *before* you were born, and it will continue for the rest of your life, or theirs, whoever kicks the bucket first. You're never so old or so competent or so successful that your parents stop worrying about you. Worry is simply part of a parent's job description. If they didn't worry, they wouldn't be very good parents. If and when you have kids of your own, you'll know what I mean.

It's easy to see why parents worry about little kids. Children are always doing incredibly bright things like walking out in front of cars, falling into swimming pools, sticking metal objects into light sockets, and eating rat poison. When you were a little kid, your parents worried primarily about keeping you alive.

But you're not a little kid anymore. So they should stop worrying, right? Wrong, anxiety-breath. Now that you're older, you give them even more stuff to worry about.

Take your future, for example. Parents know from experience that what you do (or don't do) during your teen years has a huge impact on the rest of your life. That's why they harp incessantly on issues like homework, chores, eating right, friends, dating, entertainment, and so on. They have high hopes for you and want you to stay healthy, get an education, choose a career, and be as successful in life as you can possibly be. They don't want to find you someday picking aluminum cans out of trash bins so that you can retread the tires on your shopping cart.

They also worry about losing you. They know you're growing up fast, and they can feel you pulling away from them. They may not want to let go because they're afraid you won't come back. If you sometimes feel trapped in your house, maybe it's because your parents like having you around. Seriously. They may even resent your friends and the things you want to do simply because they take you away from them. They like being your parents.

And they worry about what they don't know. This may seem ridiculous, but it's true. Parents fear the unknown. When they don't know what you're doing or where you're going, or who you're with, they fear the worst. It's easier for them to just make you stay home where they can keep an eye on you. You may be a grump, but at least they know where you are.

So give them a break. Tell them they're cute when they worry like that. Then try to unworry them by being as responsible and talkative as you possibly can. Tell them what's going on. Help them understand your world a little better. Introduce your friends to them. The less they have to worry about, the more freedom you're likely to get.

PARENTS HAVE A PILE OF PROBLEMS - - - - - - - - - -

If you take pride in being the center of attention, you may be heartbroken to learn that you are only *one* of the many problems your parents have to deal with every single day. They have a virtual plethora of problems. In fact, the older you get, the more problems you get. Now, there's something to look forward to.

You may think that being an adult is a piece of cake. *"I can't wait until I'm an adult. Then life will be perfect. All my problems will go away. I'll have it all together and know exactly what to do in every situation."*

Um, HELLO! Truth is, when you become an adult, you simply trade in one set of problems for another. And thanks to a cruel twist of nature, parents of teenagers are at the age when they're probably going to get a double dose of them.

Ever heard of a midlife crisis? The name alone can depress you. If your parents are in their forties (plus or minus a few years) they are probably in the process of reexamining their lives, their dreams, their relationships, and their values. In fact, it's a lot like adolescence. Just when you're going through this big transition in your life—from childhood into adulthood—your parents run smack dab into some serious transition issues of their own. They look in the mirror, see themselves getting old and gray, and it scares them half to death.

During this time in their lives, the mere fact that they have a teenager in the house can twist the knife of midlife a little deeper into their psyches. Your youth reminds them that theirs is heading south. That's one of the reasons some parents start behaving like teenagers themselves. They develop what is known as the middle-age crazies. They may go back to school, or get a face-lift, or buy a souped-up sports car, or get a new job. Some parents try to live their lives through their kids and put pressure on them to become something that they (the parents) never had the chance to be.

Even more surprising, some parents going through midlife become jealous of their teenagers. They may be jealous of all the options you still have open to you when they realize that those options are closed to them. They may be jealous of your dreams. They remember having dreams of their own; but the realities of life forced them to put those dreams on hold, and now they seem impossible. Your dad may now realize he'll never own his own business, or become a professional ball player, or live in a house on the beach. Your mom may have held out for years to finish her education, or to become a lawyer, or a concert pianist, but time is slipping away.

Your mom and dad may not be having a midlife crisis, but they're probably facing other problems that create stress and add pressure to their relationship with you and the whole family. Let's take a look at the sidebar and just a few of the problems your parents might be dealing with right now.

Physical problems. Even if your parents are relatively healthy, they may worry a lot more about their health now that they see more people their age having serious health problems, and even dying.

Financial problems. Unless your parents are very wealthy, they're probably under a lot of financial pressure right now. When you became a teenager, all their expenses increased. Your folks may worry that they haven't done a very good job of saving for college or for their own retirement. And if the economy isn't doing well, family finances are even more stressful.

Job problems. Maybe your parents have problems at work that impact your family. They may have grown unhappy with what they do for a living and wish they could change it. Maybe they were laid off or experienced a business failure. Maybe they feel guilt or exhaustion from working long hours. Maybe they are angry with a boss or coworker and take it out on you. I remember one day a few years ago when some job-related problems were getting me down, and I opened up my briefcase to find a handmade card from my daughter Amber. In it she wrote, "Dad, I know things are hard for you right now. I want you to know that I love you, and I'm praying for you today." Believe me, that note made all my problems go away, at least for that day.

Family problems. It's possible that your parents are at the age when they have to provide assistance or care for their own parents. Other problems with your extended family may have spilled over into yours.

Personal problems. Your parents may struggle with personal issues such as changes in their weight, appearance, and sexual vitality.

Emotional problems. To repeat what I wrote earlier, your parents have feelings just like you do. But they may also have emotional or psychological problems that require special understanding or medical treatment.

It's also common for people in their middle years to have bouts with clinical depression (which can usually be treated with medication).

As your parents get older, they will undoubtedly experience a few hormonal changes that will cause them to act a bit...well...weird.

Your mom, for example, may have a temporary case of PMS (pre-menstrual syndrome). This can cause her to be irritable and extremely emotional. Try not to take anything directed at you too personally.

And then there's menopause. This is common with women during mid-life.

Dads also can go through a kind of male menopause (sometimes called andropause) which affects them in much the same way as their wives. Again, just give your Dad some space if he seems extra grumpy or preoccupied with himself.

If it's sometimes difficult to talk with your parents about the problems you're facing, the same is probably true for your parents. They may feel uncomfortable telling you about their problems and the things they're going through. Sometimes they keep it all to themselves because they love you and don't want to burden you or make you worry. Sometimes they just want to create the illusion that everything's okay, for your sake..

Don't expect your parents to tell you everything, but know your parents often have many pressing concerns that will impact how they treat you amd communicate with you. You need to be understanding and patient during these times. You don't need to know all the detials and you certainly don't need to be put on the postion of a counselor or therapist for your parents, but you can give them some space and try not to add fuel to the fire.

One other thing you can do, and it's the most important of all. *Pray for your parents.* Ask God to give them strength, guidance, courage, comfort, and healing while they deal with the problems they face right now. With God's help, your mom and dad will be able to survive the problems of parenthood...and so will you.

PARENTS LOVE YOU MORE THAN YOU REALIZE - - - - - -

You probably expected I'd get to this one sooner or later. But it really is true. Most of us never realize how much our parents love us until much later, when we have kids of our own. Then we understand a little better what a parent's love is all about.

"But if they love me so much, why do they make my life so miserable?"

Well, parents often have a hard time expressing love to their teenagers. When you were little, it was a lot easier. They could hold you and hug you and plant wet kisses all over your face. You probably don't let them do that anymore. But they love you just the same.

Your parents may show their love now by doing things for you or giving you things. But they also show their love by *not* doing everything for you or not giving you everything you want. They do this because they don't want you to grow up to be irresponsible or think that everything can be had for free. Believe me, they love the good feeling that comes from taking care of you and giving you gifts; but because they love you even more, they show some restraint and try not to do too much.

And they show their love when they provide discipline when you need it. You've probably heard the old line, "This is going to hurt me more than it does you." Usually you hear that just before you get whacked. But there's a lot of truth to it. Parents don't derive some ghoulish pleasure out of punishing their kids or putting them on restriction. But they sometimes do it because they love you.

I mentioned this earlier, but it's worth repeating. The greater the love and commitment family members have, the greater the possibility for conflict and hurt. It's precisely because your parents love you so much that they risk making you angry and upset with them. I've worked with teenagers for many years and I've watched a few kids do things that I knew they'd regret later. I did very little to stop them, even when I could. Yes, I cared about them, but I didn't care enough or love them enough to risk making them angry with me. My own kids, on the other hand, were angry with me a lot. They didn't think I was nearly as cool as the kids in my youth group did. That's because I didn't really care if my children liked me all the time. I loved them too much.

Remember that God our Father in Heaven only disciplines those whom he loves. If God doesn't discipline you, the Bible tells us, then you aren't his true child. "No discipline seems pleasant at the time, but painful. But later on, it produces a harvest of righteousness and peace for those who have been trained by it" (Hebrews 12:11). God loves you and so do your parents. Be thankful that they love you enough to give you the training you need.

> *My parents and I have a good relationship, but not to the extent that I go to them with all my problems. They will often ask me about what I'm doing, and that helps me know how much they care.*
>
> —Ben, age 18

GAME OVER!

(HOW TO BLOW IT BIG TIME WITH YOUR PARENTS)

Okay, now that we've defined what a parent is and what a parent isn't, it's time to talk about YOU. What can *you* do to live happily ever after with your mom and dad?

Well, let's hold off on that question for one more chapter. Right now, I want you to take a close look at just a few of the ways you can totally blow it with your parents. Then in Chapter Four I'll give you some ways to be the perfect teenager and totally blow your parents' minds.

Maybe a word to the wise is in order here. You don't want to get this chapter confused with the next one. THIS chapter is a list of things to NOT do. These are BAD IDEAS. I repeat: DO NOT TRY THESE AT HOME. If you do, I cannot be held responsible.

And why do we waste paper on stuff like this? Because the first step toward doing the right things is to stop doing the wrong things. And if you don't know what the wrong things are, you can't stop doing them. So read on. This list isn't complete, of course. I'm sure you can think of other ways to mess up your life besides these.

THINK LIKE A LOSER – – – – – – – –

How Losers Think
  "MY parents hate me."
  "I can't do anything right."
  "Nobody understands me."
  "What I do doesn't make any difference."
  "You can't tell me what to do."

Just commit a few of the uplifting, happy thoughts in the sidebar to memory, and you can go straight to the head of the class. You don't need to do much else to permanently keep the relationship you have with your folks in the dumpster. Think like a loser, and you'll end up a loser. Smart people have known this for a long, long time (see Proverbs 23:7).

You know it too. If you play sports, for example, you know

you aren't going to win if you start out thinking you're going to lose. You'll find a way to lose, no matter what.

In the same dumb way, if your mind is made up that life is going to be miserable at home and that mom and dad are the enemy and you can't do anything to change your situation, you may as well move your game piece straight to Loserville. Nothing can help you, not even all the incredible wisdom in this book. As long as you think of yourself as a lost cause, you're toast.

I know it's easier to have a bad attitude about your parents than a good one. And it's probably a lot more socially acceptable. Who wants to have a good relationship with their parents, anyway? Only dorks do that. Interestingly enough, kids who say that are the same kids who don't have a problem taking their parents' money, eating their food, living in their house, using their credit cards, driving their cars...but hey, at least they aren't dorks. What they don't know is...you don't have to be a dork to be a loser.

Look, you don't have to give up your coolness to stay on your parents' good side. You don't have to dress like them, talk like them, act like them, or even hang out with them too much. There's nothing dorky about being smart enough to realize that the relationship you have with your parents is the most important relationship you'll ever have with anybody. You want them to be on your side. They, after all, make decisions about your freedom. Someday they'll also make decisions about your *inheritance*. It might be a good idea to think a little more long-term than next weekend.

PRETEND YOU KNOW MORE THAN THEY DO

Trust me on this one. Not only do you not know *more* than your parents, you don't even know *as much*. Please don't take this personally, Einstein. It has nothing to do with you or your intelligence (which is obviously high or you wouldn't be reading this book.). It's just that you can't possibly know (yet) what your parents know. Despite their ignorance of pop culture, they still have an advantage over you in the knowledge department simply because they have been alive at least twice as long as you. Believe it or not, experience is an incredible teacher of life's deepest mysteries.

I know it's a pain when your parents harp on stuff you already know. But sometimes they forget that they told you a thousand times already to put on some sunscreen when you go outside. They just want to impress upon you that a great tan isn't worth the inconvenience of skin cancer on your nose. They've had enough trips to the dermatologist to know this is absolutely true. But, do *you* understand that? They aren't so sure.

Parents have a way different perspective than you do. Even when you're sure they're flat-out wrong and have no idea what they're talking about, it's probably just a matter of perspective. They see things differently because they have more life experiences to help them interpret what they see. What seems totally okay to you may look terrible to your parents because they've seen this scenario before.

Ever hear of 20/20 hindsight? They say everybody's got it. It's the ability to know what to do *after* something happens rather than *before*. If you said after the geometry test, "Golly gee whillikers, I should have studied up a little more on that Pythagorean theorem stuff," that's 20/20 hindsight. Obviously, you would have been better off if this light came on BEFORE the test. Well, it's the same deal with parents and all their nagging. They've been around the block a few times, and they want to save you the hassle of making all the same dumb mistakes they made.

It won't do any good, of course. You'll make your share of mistakes just like they did and share your vast wisdom with your kids. But here's an even better reason to not treat your parents as if they're your intellectual inferiors. If you learn to appreciate and respect what your parents have to say, they may be more inclined to give you the keys to the car. They'll notice your humility and respect and bestow upon you more privileges and freedom than you might otherwise receive. Parents like to feel good about themselves too, and quite often they will reward those who make them feel a little smarter.

IF YOU DON'T GET YOUR WAY, GET MAD

I was in a restaurant a few months ago enjoying a nice peaceful dinner with my wife when I noticed a family sitting at a table about 20 feet away. Seated around the table were a dad, a mom, and three kids, one of them a girl about 15 years old. I wouldn't have paid any attention to them except that they were having a rather heated discussion. I'm not sure what was going on or what was being said, but all of a sudden the daughter stood up, threw her silverware down on the table, screamed a few choice phrases at her parents that made everyone in the restaurant blush, and ran out of the room. Her father calmly apologized to the waiter and went outside to find his daughter. The rest of the family remained at the table for several minutes in stunned silence, obviously very embarrassed. I felt embarrassed for them too, even though I didn't know them at all. Their little family outing ended in disaster.

As I said, I don't know the cause of the problem—but whatever it was, I doubt very much that the tantrum-throwing young lady who exploded in anger that night did much to help her cause. Maybe she just wanted to make sure her parents would stay mad at her for the next 30 years. If so, she probably got her wish. What she didn't understand is that when you accuse your parents of being the worst bleeping parents in the world in front of an audience of 50 or 60 people, your parents are not likely to forget that episode for a long, long time. If she'd done a better job of controlling her anger and calmly talking to her parents about the situation later, she would likely be enjoying her freedom right now. My guess is that she's either still grounded or serving a sentence somewhere in Colorado in one of those institutions for wayward girls with Attila the Headmaster making up all the rules.

Parents generally don't respond very well to an angry teenager. You yell at them; they yell back. And, more often than not, they'll take action that will further dampen your spirits. Remember, they hold all the cards. Blow up at them, and they'll blow up your plans for the weekend. When you unleash hostility on your parents, they have no alternative but to punish you. Believe me, they would rather not, which is why it's in your own best interests to calm down and try to solve the problem peacefully. You may not like the idea of apologizing or admitting that you're wrong, but the sooner you let go of your anger, the sooner they will let you get on with your happy, fun-loving life.

While we're on the subject, let me give you a little advice on the words you use. You do not ever want to use swear words, especially those top-of-the-line varsity swear words that are still not allowed on prime-time TV. Suddenly the argument or the infraction will take on added depth and seriousness. Trust me; don't do this. Secondly, never ever call your mother or father a derogatory name. Calling your parents names or heaping slurs upon their heritage never gets you anywhere. You end up being the butthead, not them. Third, do not threaten your parents, ever. Threatening your parents is like waving a red flag in front of a bull. Threats shift the argument to a no-win power struggle where both sides feel backed into a corner. Besides, what can you threaten them with? *"Then I'll just starve myself!" "Then I just won't go to the party!" "Then I'll flunk the class on purpose!"* You may think your parents are really worried, but ultimately you're the one who ends up hungry, with no social life, and a class to make up in summer school. The whole point was to get back at your parents, but all you've done is mess up your own life.

Check out the sidebar for some other dumb things you want to stop before they come out of your mouth.

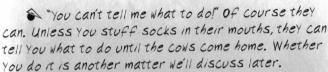

🔖 "You can't tell me what to do!" Of course they can. Unless you stuff socks in their mouths, they can tell you what to do until the cows come home. Whether you do it is another matter we'll discuss later.

🔖 "You can't make me do it!" True. They know they can't. But why do you want to get into a power struggle that you just can't win? This is like purposely diving into a swimming pool full of piranhas.

🔖 "I didn't ask to be born!" Well, don't push your luck. You might have been turned down. The point is moot now anyway, isn't it?

🔖 "But _____'s parents let him do it!" This usually gets the same response from your parents that you give when they say, "Eat your dinner because children are starving in Africa." Yawn. Big who cares? What does eating dinner have to do with children starving in Africa? Nothing that you can figure out. Are you supposed to mail your dinner to the starving children or what? In the same way, your parents really don't see the point. They will probably say, "Well, we're not _____'s parents and you're not _____." End of discussion.

🔖 "I don't care." Yes you do, and your parents know you do. This accomplishes nothing, and if your parents actually believe you, you've given them permission to do whatever they want to you. If you care, which you probably do, you should try to work with your parents to find a solution.

I know it's impossible to never be mad at your parents.

When they don't give you what you want, or discipline you for something you did, or say something cruel and insensitive, you naturally feel ticked off or hurt. That's okay. You don't have to be a happy camper 24 hours a day. But don't let your anger make you do something stupid. The Bible says, "In your anger do not sin" (Ephesians 4:26).

And here's a little extra advice. If and when you get mad, don't stay mad. Get over it as quickly as you can. "Don't let the sun go down while you are still angry" is how the Bible puts it (Ephesians 4:26). The longer you stay mad, the longer your parents will be reminded that you broke the rules. The longer you hold a grudge against your parents, the longer it will take to improve your living conditions. On top of that, a permanent frown doesn't do much for your looks.

IF YOU DISAGREE, DISOBEY – – – – – –

This one reminds me of the time I borrowed the family car to cruise the boulevard one Friday night when I was sixteen years old. My parents were going out for the evening with some friends, and they gave me strict instructions to stay home. But dang it anyway, I wanted to go out. I had a brand-new driver's license, and I wanted to put it to good use. I wasn't going to do anything wrong. But N-O, they said. They didn't think I was ready to be out driving at night, especially if I didn't need to go anywhere in particular. They seemed satisfied that I got the message and was going to stay home.

But as soon as they were gone, I began weighing the evidence. Since my parents left the car sitting right there in the garage, and since I had a valid California driver's license, and since I knew where the extra set of car keys were, and since I knew I could make it up and down the boulevard (a distance of less than 3 miles) and get back in plenty of time, and since I considered my parents' instructions to be extremely unreasonable and unfair, I knew what I had to do. I decided to live dangerously. No one would ever know.

To make a long story short, everything went just fine except for that guy in the '59 El Camino who decided to stop suddenly in front of me. I had a little problem finding the brake pedal, and the next thing I knew the hood on my parents' new car looked like an accordion. Needless to say, I got my driver's license suspended by my parents, and I got a big fat bill for auto repairs to pay off in weekly installments out of the pittance they called my allowance.

But even worse than being grounded and broke, my parents for some reason had a hard time believing me like they did before. It took me forever to prove to them that they could trust me again.

I've seen this same scenario play itself out with lots of teenagers over the years. It's a lesson that some kids never learn. No matter how clever you think you are, disobedience rarely turns out to be worth the hassle. It's a lousy deal with the devil that almost always sabotages your freedom and undermines your relationship with your parents.

When you disregard your parents' wishes and betray them with disobedience, you may get what you want for a while—but you'll find that the price you pay is a high one. Even when you think you're getting away with it, your parents wise up pretty quickly and clamp down more, not less.

Look, when God gave us the commandment to honor and obey our parents, he had your best interests in mind. "Children, obey your parents, for this is right. Honor your father and your mother"—which is the first commandment with a promise. And what is the promise? "That it may go well with you and that you may enjoy long life on the earth" (Ephesians 6:1-3). Any questions?

IF THEY GIVE YOU AN INCH, TAKE A MILE

Here's another privilege-killer. Whenever your parents agree to something, take a little (or a lot) more. Stick it to them! Check out the sidebar for a few ideas.

How to Stick It to 'Em

🔥 If they let you use their credit card to go to the mall and buy school clothes, pick up a few DVDs and CDs while you're at it. They'll never notice the extra charges, right?

🔥 If they give you a cell phone, ignore the 300 free minutes you get on the plan, and run up the phone bill. You can just tell them you didn't realize your friends talked so long. You'll try to do better next month, heh heh.

🔥 If they let you stay out until 11:00, stay out until 12:00. What's another hour? Besides, you can give them a lame excuse about your suicidal friend who really needed someone to talk to. You couldn't just leave her, could you?

🔥 If they let you postpone a chore you don't like to do until tomorrow, pretend to forget about it, and don't do it at all.

You get the picture. Kids do this kind of stuff all the time to their parents, and then they wonder why mom and dad aren't more willing to give them what they want. Don't be that stupid. You may think you're pulling one off on your parents but all you're doing is killing the goose that lays the golden eggs. They'll eventually stop giving you anything at all. Can you blame them?

An old proverb says, "It's impossible to steal as much as you can earn." Why steal from your parents when, by earning their trust, they will probably give you what you want anyway? It really doesn't make much sense. Why blow the whole future for a little extra fun today? It reminds me of the story Jesus told about the boy who demanded his inheritance in advance from his father, and then he took off with the money and lived like a selfish pig. He really thought he was living the good life until he ran out of cash. It wasn't until then that he realized what a jerk he had been. He knew his father would have given him anything he wanted, but nooooo—he had to do it his way.

The happy ending of that story, in case you don't know it, has the boy getting a lavish welcome home party thrown by his father who loves him in spite of his foolishness (Luke 15:11-32). Maybe your parents are like that, but don't push your luck. Jesus told the story to tell us what God is like, not your mom and dad. Your parents may love you no matter what, but they will be hurt and less trustful of you if you abuse their love and take advantage of their generosity. If they give you an inch, say thank you and be responsible with it.

LIE YOUR WAY OUT OF TROUBLE

This is another popular teen defense mechanism that never works. Lying to your parents to save your own skin always backfires and creates more problems than it solves. Still, lots of kids live by an unwritten code of parent communication that goes something like the list in the sidebar.

Communication for Dummies
1. *Avoid talking to your parents.*
2. *If you must talk to your parents, be as evasive as possible.*
3. *Only admit to the stuff they already know.*
4. *Lie about everything else.*

Why is this sidebar list a strategy for dummies? First off, if you give your parents the silent treatment, you'll only prompt them to ask a lot more questions. Do you like hearing more questions? Sure, about as much as you like the sound of fingernails scratching a blackboard.

Second, if you're evasive and keep them in the dark, you'll only prolong the pain.

Where are you going?
Out.
Out where?
Just out.
Why won't you tell me where you're going?
Just out, mom. Do you have to know everything?
No, I don't have to know everything. I just want to know where you're going.
Out.
Out WHERE?
Why do you have to know where I'm going anyway? Don't you trust me?
Jon, if you don't tell me now where you're going, you're not going anywhere.
I'm going OUT!

See what I mean? This conversation could go on for days.

Third, if you only admit to what parents already know, they'll wonder what they don't know and assume it's bad.

Fourth, lying is, to use a metaphor, handing your parents the rope that you'll soon be hanging from.

I know, when parents start asking questions, you feel threatened. You may get the feeling that you are being interrogated for a crime or that your parents are looking for some way to vote you out of the family as...*the weakest link!* But if you conceal the truth or lie, that's not a good strategy for stopping the questions. You'll only get more questions, more frequently.

Here's a little secret. The more your parents trust you, the less they'll have to give you the third degree every time you want to do something. If you have a history of being open and honest with them, they won't worry so much about what you're doing. Sometimes it's worry and distrust that makes them ask all those annoying questions that make you feel like you're being grilled.

Jason could have avoided a lot of questions if he hadn't tried to pull a fast one on his folks:

Dad: "Jason, you said you were going to Nick's house. Why didn't you call and tell us that you were going to a party at Carrie's? You know the rules."

Jason: "But dad, I tried to call. Twice. The line was busy. I didn't know what to do. I thought it would be okay. I didn't know her parents weren't going to be home. And I wasn't drinking. Only Nick was."

Dad: "Jason, we weren't on the phone. You didn't try to call us."

Jason: "Yes I did. Maybe the phone was left off the hook."

Dad: "The phone was not off the hook. And besides, you knew we wouldn't have let you go to that party. How can you stand there and lie to us!"

Jason: "You don't believe anything I say! You never trust me!"

Sorry, Jason, but you lose. You were caught in a lie. *"But they can't prove I was lying."* Doesn't matter. Your parents know you lied to them, and now you have an even bigger problem. They have no choice but to doubt everything else you say. Do you really think they believe you weren't drinking? Of course not! But that's not their problem; it's yours.

Like Jason, when you deceive your parents—regardless of how clever you are—you're likely to be found out. No, your parents don't have built-in BS detectors, and they may not find out every detail of your deception, but they'll know they've been had.

And they will almost always find it a lot harder to forgive the lying than they do whatever it is you're lying about.

"*But I don't lie. I just don't tell them everything.*" Come on. You know you don't have to make up fairy tales to be a liar. When you secretly disobey your parents, tell them half-truths, leave out relevant information they need, or otherwise mislead them, you're guilty of parent perjury. It still means you can't be trusted.

At least be honest with yourself, if you can't be honest with your parents. Do you want people to trust you and give you the respect you deserve? Do you want people to treat you more like an adult and less like a child? Do you want your nose to stop growing? Then do yourself a favor, and stop yourself next time you're tempted to try to put one over on your folks.

Your parents want to believe everything you say—they really do. They know you're not perfect, so they don't expect perfection. They know you're going to mess up from time to time. But when you try to hide your shortcomings by lying to them, you tell them that you don't believe they love you enough to accept you the way you are. That hurts. What hurts even more is when you take away their ability to trust you.

The Bible has lots to say about lying, of course, but I'll give you one verse—a prayer from Psalm 120:2. "Save me, O Lord, from lying lips and from deceitful tongues." Amen to that!

MAKE EVERYTHING BE ABOUT YOU – – – – – – – – – – – –

Want your parents to keep treating you like a child instead of a young adult? Then keep demanding the same attention you got when you were a baby. You can't blame a little child for getting cranky when he's hungry or has messed his diaper, but it's really annoying when a teenager does pretty much the same thing. If you're looking for a way to suck the life out of your relationship with your parents, make every conversation, every trip, every purchase, every everything be about you.

Mom, can you take me to Wal-Mart?

I really don't feel well, Brittany.
But I have to get some notebook paper.
Why don't you borrow some from Katie?
But she doesn't have the kind I like.
Brittany, I'm really feeling badly.
But mom, I REALLY NEED SOME NOTEBOOK PAPER!

Brittany is what we refer to as a high-maintenance teenager. She's also very selfish. She doesn't care that her mother is sick. *"But it's her job to take me where I need to go! She doesn't feel that sick. Besides, what am I supposed to do, go without notebook paper? I can't drive."* Me, me, everything is about me. I don't know about you, but I tend to avoid people like Brittany who are extremely needy, totally self-centered, impossible to please, and who take everything as a personal attack. They are relentless takers but they never give anything back. No one can ever do enough for them or like them enough. Anything that's not a compliment is an insult. Any kind of criticism causes them to either get very hurt or very mad.

Part of becoming an adult is to learn how to put the needs of others ahead of your own. In any relationship, the key to being liked and respected by others is to not require it of them. It's being humble and considerate of others.

What if Brittany said, *"Mom, I'm sorry you're not feeling well. I'll survive without notebook paper right now. You just get some rest."* Gosh, not only would Brittany's mom go out of her way to help her later on, but she would probably get well a whole lot quicker.

> **I hate when my parents pry into my life instead of letting me talk to them.**
> —Julianne, age 18

BLAME THEM FOR YOUR BEHAVIOR - - - - - - - - - - - -

They should have known I would do it.
They didn't tell me it was wrong.
But they made me so mad.
They made me run away from home.
If they hadn't been so strict, I wouldn't have gotten into so much trouble.
They didn't show me how to do it.

Give your parents a break. They may make convenient targets for the blame game, but they have nothing to do with what you decide to do, how you decide to feel, or how you decide to respond to things in your life. They are not the Great Satan who is responsible for how you choose to mess up your own life. Do they control what you do? Don't give them so much credit.

If things aren't going your way, don't blame your parents. If you're unhappy, that doesn't necessarily mean your parents caused your unhappiness. Blaming them doesn't really change the situation, does it? All it does is make you feel helpless and hopeless. Once you stop blaming them, you can do something to change the situation.

Be a grown-up. Have the guts to take responsibility for yourself and what you do. When stuff happens—whether your parents had anything to do with it or not—you have unlimited options of how to respond. If you make the right choice and do something right, take credit and build on it. If you screw things up, accept responsibility and learn from it. Regardless, leave your parents out of it. You'll be a lot happier, and so will they.

HELP YOURSELF TO THEIR STUFF - - - - - - - - - - - - - -

Just as some kids think they're not really lying when they lie to their parents, some kids think they're not really stealing when they steal from their parents. *"Sure, why not? Everything they have belongs to me anyway...I'm just getting my inheritance a little early..."*

Want another good way to make sure your parents have a hard time trusting you? Want to do something else to sabotage your relationship with them? Become a thief in your own house.

Look, parents don't have much to call their own, anyway. The house, the food, the cars, the furniture—all that stuff belongs to you and everybody else in the family even though it was bought and paid for by Mom and Dad. That makes them all the more protective of the few things they do have. You know what they are: Mom's perfume, her jewelry, her clothes, her purse and what's in it; Dad's guitar, his tools, his clothes, his wallet and what's in it. Is that too much to ask?

I know you don't like it when your brother or sister or anyone else steals from you. You feel personally violated, even when the stuff is easily replaced. Likewise, your parents have a right to expect you to leave their things alone.

Several years ago I bought a really cool sweater that I wanted to wear to a speaking engagement. I was speaking to a group of teenagers, so I knew they would think it was cool too. But the night of the speaking engagement, I couldn't find that new sweater anywhere. I knew exactly where I had put it, but it was gone. No one seemed to know anything about it. But several days later one of my kids (name withheld to protect the guilty) confessed to borrowing it. The only problem—it was left at a friend's house and apparently vanished. I never did get it back.

I still remember how frustrated and angry I got over that missing sweater. It's actually kind of embarrassing now. Of course, I wasn't that angry over losing the sweater. I had something else to wear. But it was the inconvenience of not knowing where it was and having to look all over the house for it, and feeling frustrated that *someone would do that to me.* (By the way, now you know why many parents dress like dorks. They do it so that their kids won't be tempted to borrow their clothes.)

Whether it's pilfering money out of your mom's purse or using your dad's designer after-shave lotion—if you don't get permission, don't do it. Not only is it stealing, but you are eroding your parents' trust in you. Don't mistake your parents for fools. They know what's going on, and the more you violate their privacy, the less privacy you're going to get.

PLAY ONE PARENT OFF THE OTHER - - - - - - - - - - -

"Mom, can you take me over to Sarah's house? Her mom said it was okay, and she'll give me a ride home. I'll be home by 9 o'clock. I promise.

"No, Hillary, it's a school night, and you have homework to do.

"But mom, I just have a little homework, and I can do it when I get home."

"No, and that's final."

"Mom!"

A few minutes later in the garage—

"Dad, can you take me over to Sarah's house? Pretty please? Her mom said it was okay, and she'll bring me home by 9. Mom's busy.

"What about your homework?"

"I told mom that I would do it when I got home. I don't have much."

"I guess I can do that. Let me get my car keys."

Hillary is a devious parent manipulator who thinks she's pretty clever to not mention a rather important detail about her earlier conversation with mom. In her view, she didn't actually *lie*. She just put in a second request to parent #2 and took a chance that her dad might unwittingly veto parent #1's decision. *Bingo*. She was right.

Of course, what Hillary didn't hear was the big argument that took place a little later between Mom and Dad when Mom found out that Hillary was gone. Not wanting to admit he'd had been had, Dad lamely tried to justify his decision to let his daughter go to Sarah's. Mom ended up furious with both Dad *and* Hillary.

Sometimes called Parent Ping Pong, this is a deadly game, and everybody loses. Don't play it. Not only will you get busted, you'll risk undermining your parents' marriage. You don't want to move on to the Visiting-Dad-on-Weekends game.

Now if your parents are already divorced, you have a tremendous advantage in this game. They may not be able to work together to provide the discipline that you need and neither of them wants to be the bad guy. That makes it a lot easier for you to play one against the other. Some kids become rather skilled at manipulating their divorced parents and getting what they want. But kids who do this are selfish, mean-spirited, and very shortsighted. Both parents know they are being betrayed, and they know who is setting them up. They may feel helpless, but they aren't stupid. Ultimately you will be the one who suffers as you lose the trust of the two people who love you the most.

It's okay to thoughtfully consider which parent will be most lenient or cut you the most slack. There's nothing dishonest about knowing how to play your cards well. Choose the parent you think will offer you the best chance of success, and then go ask. There's no point in asking Dad if you know already that he won't let you do it. Better off asking Mom. But here's the rule: you only get one shot. Make it count. You can't ask one parent and then go try the other if you lose on the first try. They won't like that; and in the end, you'll lose even more.

ROCK THE HOUSE

(HOW TO SCORE POINTS WITH YOUR PARENTS AND LIVE HAPPILY EVER AFTER)

Now we get to the good stuff. Everything else has just been a setup for this chapter. You want to do the things to have a rock-solid relationship with your folks. Whether you're punk or preppie, hip or hokey, chic or geek, these strategies will work for you. Regardless of your race, creed, or color, these ideas will help you survive and thrive in your home sweet home. Whether you have one parent, two parents, four parents, or 20 parents—you'll learn how to get them off your back and get yourself a lot more trust, more freedom, and greater responsibility.

But let me warn you—it's not going to be easy. This chapter is not for wimps. You'll notice that it's longer and tougher. But it's going to be worth it. So buckle up. Strap it down. Turn off all pagers and cell phones. Pay close attention, let your brain marinate in all the good ideas you find on the next few pages...then go rock your house!

BE A THERMOSTAT, NOT A THERMOMETER

Do things sometimes get a little heated up in your house? You can turn the temperature down, you know. But to do that, you have to be a thermostat, not a thermometer. Know the difference?

A thermostat is a pretty powerful piece of equipment. It controls the temperature in the room. It's an instrument of change. Turn it up, and the temperature goes up. Turn it down, and the temperature goes down. Sweet.

But a thermometer is different. It has no power at all. It merely responds to the temperature in the room. It can tell you how hot or how cold things get, but it can't do much of anything else. It doesn't change the temperature; the temperature changes it. It is at the mercy of its surroundings.

Now, in your family, you can either be a thermostat or a thermometer. You can either be an instrument of change or a victim of circumstances. You can either *describe* what happens to you, or you can *decide* what happens to you. It's totally up to you.

If you've read this far, I'm guessing that you don't want to be just a thermometer. You want a better relationship with your parents, and you're willing to do something about it. Rather than wishing and waiting for good things to happen, you're willing to take some steps to *make* good things happen. You do want to be a thermostat, don't you?

Then let God use you. As you probably realize, you can't do any of this stuff alone. But with God's help you can do anything he wants you to do. And he definitely wants to use you to change things in your family. That's why he put this book into your hands. You don't have to believe in yourself or your ability to do anything at all. Just believe that he can do it all through you.

If you need a little inspiration, read the story of David and Goliath in 1 Samuel 17. David decided to be a thermostat, while Saul's army was content to be a bunch of thermometers. All they did was watch. But David, the teenager, boldly picked up his slingshot and went out to face the giant. He didn't even bother to wear armor. When the soldiers insisted that he was too small to beat a huge giant like Goliath, David knew that God would deliver the giant into his hands (17:46). That gave him the courage and determination to do what no one else thought he could do.

You can do the same thing in your family. Keep on reading, and let God use you to make a big difference in your family.

- - - - - - - CHANGE YOURSELF FIRST

For a thermostat to change the temperature in a room, the first thing the thermostat needs is to adjust itself. The setting has to be changed.

In the same way, remember that you can't try to change your parents or change your family or change anything else but yourself. When *you* change in a positive direction, you'll start to see other positive changes happen around you.

What are some of the changes you would like to see in your parents? Do you want them to give you more freedom? Want them to trust you more? Want them to stop nagging so much? Well, you can't do much to control any of those things. All you can do is change you.

A little parable

Once upon a time, a man set out to change the world. But it didn't take long for him to discover that the world was far too big for one person to change.

So he decided to change his country. But after a while, he discovered that countries don't change when crooked politicians and special interest groups run them.

So he decided to change his neighborhood. But his neighbors wouldn't cooperate. They simply closed their doors and shut their windows.

So he decided to change his family. But when he tried to change his family, his children rebelled, his wife went into therapy, and things only got worse.

Finally, the man decided to change himself.

And when he did that, he was able to change the world.

From this point on, I'm going to give you some ways to change yourself. All of these suggestions require you to do some things you may never have done before. They may require you to change your attitude, your perspective, or your behavior. But do them, and watch what happens. You'll begin to notice other people around you start to change too.

SWEAT THE SMALL STUFF - - - - - - - -

You've heard the phrase, "Don't sweat the small stuff." That's good advice...sometimes. But let's face it. Sometimes it's the small stuff that can make or break a relationship. Sure, big stuff is important, but it's also...well...big. Its bigness can make it so overwhelming that you can't do anything about it. Small stuff, on the other hand, is manageable. And it's a good place to start if you want to improve your relationship with your parents.

For example, I show my wife that I love her by being faithful to her (big stuff). But if I lift the lid on the toilet seat and don't put it back down when I'm through (small stuff), she may question my love for her, even though I'm faithful as a puppy. I've heard of marriages that fell apart because somebody failed to squeeze the toothpaste from the right end of the tube or didn't put their dirty clothes in the hamper or forgot to bring flowers on their anniversary or cooked the eggs too hard. This is all small stuff, but it can sometimes create big problems between people who aren't doing too badly in the big-stuff department.

You may be doing great with the big stuff—you don't do drugs, you aren't getting wasted at parties, you aren't doing anything immoral or illegal. But how are you doing with the small stuff? What are the recurring hassles at home that seem stupid but cause all kinds of problems between you and your parents? If you'll take the initiative to eliminate them, your life (and theirs) will get a whole lot easier. Here are some examples.

Your bedroom. I'm not sure why this is such a big hang-up for parents. It's as if they think there's a commandment in the Bible that says, "Thou shalt clean thy room." They worry that you won't get your mansion in heaven if you can't even make your bed! Why is this such a big deal? Does having a messy room mean you're a bad person? Of course not. In reality, it's a small thing. But if it's a big thing to your mom or dad, then you are wise to make it a big thing too. Try to get up a little earlier than usual for a few days and straighten things up before you leave for school. Is that so hard? Give it a try, and watch how generous and loving your parents suddenly become.

> *I really love my parents, but we seem to be growing apart. I think it's my fault because I'm becoming a teenager.*
> —Kristy, age 13

Chores. What chores are you expected to do? Gotta take out the trash? Mow the lawn? Feed the pets? If you've developed a serious chore allergy, join the club. Nobody likes to do chores, including your parents. So think of them as contributions to the family. Somebody in your house has got to wash, iron, and fold your clothes, prepare the meals, do the dishes, vacuum the carpets, scrub the floors, weed the garden, polish the brass, wash the car, rake the leaves, clean the toilets, shovel the snow, remove dust from the furniture, and…well, it gets depressing, doesn't it? A lot has to be done. Are you old enough and strong enough to pull your own weight around the house? Why not chip in a little more than you do right now? If you see something that needs to be done, volunteer to do it. Show your parents you're a team player and you don't expect to get everything for free. Besides, some day you'll probably have a house of your own, and it doesn't hurt to know how to do stuff like this—at least until your kids are old enough to help out like you did.

Homework. If homework is a big hassle around your house, you can make it go away by figuring out some way to get it done—before you do anything else. I realize you probably have much more important things to do, like hanging out with your friends, listening to music, talking on the phone, watching TV, eating snacks, playing video games, and so on; but the longer you put off homework, the more ominous things get around the house. Why not set aside an hour or two every afternoon to do your homework and just get it over with so Mom and D(and therefore you) can cross it off their list of things to nag you about? It's a little thing, it really is.

Your plans. You have your own life to live, right? You have things to do, places to go, people to see, parties to attend. It can be real annoying when parents put the kibosh on *your* plans because they have plans of their own, which include your staying home to baby-sit your little sister while they go out. You can save yourself a lot of hassles, not to mention a crimp on your social life, by discussing your plans ahead of time with Mom and Dad and requesting permission (rather than demanding) to do the things you want to do. That gives them time to consider your request and possibly find a substitute baby sitter. This is especially important if you need them to provide transportation for you or to provide financial backing for your plans. Plan your schedule in advance, and keep them informed. And don't forget to plan some time for them.

TEACH THEM HOW YOU WANT TO BE TREATED

Do your parents sometimes treat you like a child?

Well, it won't do any good to tell them to stop. You'll only make things worse if you stomp your feet, whine, go on a hunger strike, or throw a tantrum. As long as you act like a child, they'll treat you like one.

But there is an alternative. What you need to do is to *act the age you want them to treat you.* This will actually teach them how you want to be treated.

You're probably sick and tired of hearing your parents say, *"Act your age!"* That's because you aren't sure HOW to act. What do they expect? Just exactly how is a 13-year-old or a 15-year-old or an 18-year-old *supposed* to act? If you don't know, they probably don't know either.

Think about that. Why not pick an age that's a little older than you actually are, and try to behave like that? I'm not saying you should do the *bad things* that some older people do (like drinking, smoking, having sex, or going to R-rated movies), but do the *good things* that some older people do (like taking responsibility for yourself, being courteous and respectful around other adults, and taking your schoolwork seriously).

Like it or not, the way others treat you, including your parents, has a lot to do with how you act around them. For example, if you looked and acted like, say, a *clown*—with floppy feet, blue hair, and a big red nose—people probably wouldn't take you too seriously. In the same way, if you act like a little kid—being irresponsible all the time, pouting when you don't get your way, only caring about yourself, or avoiding anything that isn't fun—people will probably just treat you like a little kid.

And vice versa. If people treat you like a little kid, you may find yourself acting like a little kid, even though you're not.

Unfortunately, this is one of those vicious circles somebody needs to break, and it may as well be you. If you're tired of being treated like a little kid, whose fault is it? Who needs to change, them or you?

When people are around you, they pick up certain "vibes" or cues that determine how they respond to you. I'll give you a personal example of what I'm talking about. If you know me, you're aware that I am, well, follicly challenged. I started losing hair on the top of my head in my twenties. I was distressed at the time, and I tried various hair-growing remedies, none of which did any good. However, I discovered that baldness at an early age did have an upside. Many people thought I was older (and a lot wiser) than I actually was. Because of this, I was treated differently than other guys my age who looked a lot younger. People opened doors for me, called me "sir," and listened to what I had to say. I got extra respect, which felt pretty good. I decided to just go with it and do my best to play the role of a genuine adult.

Now I'm not recommending that you shave your head or anything like that. I'm just suggesting you consider how you present yourself to other people, especially your parents. Do you want them to treat you less like a child and more like an adult? Then you need to teach them how to treat you by *acting* less like a child and more like the adult (or at least growing-up) person you perceive yourself to be.

If your parents are typical, they'll continue to treat you like a child for as long as they can. They'll never stop thinking of themselves as your parents. Even when you become old enough to get senior discounts, your mom will still be tempted to wipe that smudge off your face with her hanky or nag you about eating right. After all, she still has your baby pictures hanging on the wall. She still remembers rocking you to sleep, changing your diapers, and feeding you Gerber. You may be a legal, card-carrying adult, but Mom and Dad will still have a hard time visualizing you as one.

So make it a little easier for them. Don't act like a little kid. Don't talk like a little kid. Show them you can handle more responsibility. Don't expect them to do everything for you. Speak to them in complete sentences. *Act your age.* Before you know it, they'll get the picture and realize that you're growing up after all.

MAKE REGULAR DEPOSITS TO YOUR TRUST FUND

Did you know you have a trust fund? You do! It may be small, or it may be large. But there's no doubt about it—the bigger it is, the more freedom, independence, and respect you'll have! Of course, we're not talking about a trust fund with dollars in it. We're talking about a trust fund that gets Mom and Dad to say, *"Sure, go ahead and take the car. Have a good time!"* The bigger your trust fund is, the more you'll hear things like that. But when your trust fund is too small, you're more likely to hear, *"You want to drive what? We can't even trust you to ride your bicycle without crashing it into something!"*

You may be tired of hearing about trust at this point in this book, but it's extremely important. Just as you need oxygen to breathe, you need trust to get along with your parents. You have to be able to trust them, and they have to be able to trust you.

Think of it this way. Trust is like a bridge. It connects you and your parents. It allows good communication, good feelings, and closeness. It shows faith in another person's judgment and his basic integrity. You can't have a good relationship without the bridge of trust.

I have a good relationship with my parents. They trust me, and I believe they are proud of who I have become. —Josh, age 18

So what you want to do is strengthen that bridge as much as you can. If it's really strong, you can blow it once in a while, and your parents will still trust you. You can still get over the bridge. But if it's weak to begin with, all you need is one screw-up and the bridge comes crashing down with a *"We'll never trust you again!"* Ouch.

Of course, they *will* trust you again, but only if you get to work and start making some deposits into your trust fund. Check out the sidebar for a few ways to make those deposits.

- Tell the truth. (Don't lie.)
- Respect their property. (Don't steal, and don't damage their stuff.)
- Respect their authority. (Don't be disobedient.)
- Communicate constantly. (Keep them informed, and keep things clear.)
- Admit when you're wrong. (Apologize if necessary.)
- Take responsibility for your actions. (Make restitution when you blow it.)

You can also make deposits into your trust fund by doing the other things we suggest in this chapter. It won't be easy, it will take time, and you *will* blow it on occasion. But the more deposits you make, the better position you'll be in when your fund takes a hit. You want to accumulate the largest, richest, most overflowing trust fund known in the history of home banking. It will not only pay daily dividends but it will provide a nice cushion against any possible foreclosures on your freedom.

GO THE EXTRA MILE - - - - -

Another good way to build up a positive balance in your trust fund is to do more than your parents ask you to do. Exceed expectations. Go the extra mile. If they tell you to be home by 11:00, come home at 10:30. If they ask you to carry your dishes to the sink, carry your little brother's too. If they ask you to wash the car, give it a wax job. If they expect you to get Cs on your report card, bring home a few Bs. Any time you can outperform yourself, it's like putting money in the bank.

Here's what I mean. Let's say you want to stay out later this Friday night. Since you've been coming home early, you've got some credits in your curfew account. They just might grant you an extension. And what about using the car? Since you spent so much time giving it that wax job, they just might say yes. And if your grades are better than expected, they may just let you take that part-time job you've been wanting.

Speaking of jobs, the same deal applies. If you only do the minimum that's required, your boss will probably pay you the minimum. But if you do *more*, you'll be more likely to get a raise in pay, a nice fat Christmas bonus, or a company car! You can put yourself in the driver's seat literally!

Your relationship with your parents is a lot like that. When you were a little kid, everything was one-sided. They gave; you received. They did everything; you did nothing. But now, as a teenager, there has to be some give and take. Everything is a *negotiation* (more on this later). You both

have something to give, which is what makes for a healthy relationship. The more you give, the more they will be willing to give.

This is what I think the Bible means when it says, "Honor your father and your mother." You can honor them by finding out what really floats their boat and then going out of your way to give it to them.

I remember a 16-year-old named Daniel who honored his dad by going out for football. He really didn't like football very much, but he knew that his dad did. What Daniel wanted to do was go out for golf. But because his dad had dreams of watching his son on the football field, Daniel decided to give it his best shot. As it turned out, he wasn't very good at football; and although he made the team, he only got to play when his team was either way ahead or way behind. The following year, his dad was happy to let him play golf and to support him in that.

Honor your parents by doing more and taking things further, and you can expect to get more and get further. In the Bible, Jesus taught this very same principle: "Give and it will be given to you. A good measure, pressed down, shaken together and running over, will be poured into your lap" (Luke 6:38). Give it up for your folks.

COMMIT RANDOM ACTS OF KINDNESS

While we're on the subject of giving, let me suggest a few random acts of kindness you can give your folks whenever you have the opportunity. A random act of kindness is any generous, unexpected, and unrequired activity you can perform for your parents without expecting anything in return. The sidebar has some great examples.

> Random Acts of Kindness
> - Volunteer to clean the windows in your house.
> - Buy your mom a ring or a necklace with your birthstone in it.
> - Help decorate the house for the holidays.
> - Make a big deal out of your parents' wedding anniversary.
> - Wash your parents' car.
> - Offer to help out with a financial need (if you can).

- Invite some of your friends over, and clean the house while your folks are out.
- Give your parents a welcome-home party when they come home from a trip.
- Secretly do a chore that isn't your responsibility.
- Plant some flowers in your garden, and pretend you didn't do it.
- Suggest a family outing like visiting Grandma.
- Offer to give them a day off so they can just relax (you'll take care of everything—meals, chores, laundry, etc)
- Write a letter to grandma. (She'll tell your parents about it and brag on you.)
- Have a nice portrait made of you and your brothers or sisters, and give it to your parents as a gift.
- Bring your mom or dad breakfast in bed.
- Make a handmade gift that expresses your love on Mother's or Father's Day.
- Give your parents a coupon book with things you'll do for them (like shining their shoes, doing the dishes, washing their car, etc)
- Invite your parents to chaperone a party or youth event you're going to attend.
- Ask one of your parents out on a date (dinner, movie, coffee, etc)
- Tell your parents you pray for them.
- Play a practical joke on your folks (as long as it isn't mean).
- Give them the gift of quiet.
- Offer to help with whatever they are doing at the time.

The list could go on, but you're probably feeling a little weak in the knees just from reading this far. Use your imagination, and add your own ideas.

Acts of kindness will not only make your parents' day, but you'll be investing in a savings account of goodwill you can draw on later when you want to do something. But remember these two rules: (1) Don't immediately follow up your act of kindness with a request (that's being insincere, not to mention tacky); and (2) Make sure you follow through with any offer of help you make.

GO AHEAD, BE AN EDDIE HASKELL – – – – – – – – – – – – –

Do you know who Eddie Haskell is? He's that weasel on those old *Leave it to Beaver* reruns who's known primarily for his skill at flattery. Whenever he walks in the door of Wally and Beaver's house, he says something like, "Well, hello, Mrs. Cleaver. My, but you look lovely today." And of course, a blushing Mrs. Cleaver in her apron and pearl necklace says, "Why, thank you, Eddie," and offers him a warm cookie. Eddie may not be very sincere, but he does know how to score points with parents.

Don't be afraid to be an Eddie Haskell now and then. Say something nice to your parents whenever you get the chance. They will love you for it, and you may even get more than cookies. Here's a list of suggestions. You may want to practice in the mirror first so that you don't sound completely like an idiot.

> 🖊 "Thanks a lot." Tone of voice is important with this one. Don't say it sarcastically. Or better yet, say something like, "Thanks, mom, for doing my laundry" or (after dinner) "Thanks for the great meal. I really appreciate it." Any expression of gratitude will do wonders for their self-esteem and your good standing in the home. Being thankful is the exact opposite of being a selfish pig, which is definitely something you don't want to be.

❧ "You're absolutely right." This will really disorient them. Actually, it may disorient you if
you're not used to saying it. "What did you
say?"..."I said, you're absolutely right!" and then
proceed to tell them what they are absolutely
right about. They will be amazed that you've
suddenly acquired advanced reasoning skills
and very good judgment.

❧ "I'm really proud of you." Use this on your mom
or dad, and be prepared for lots of wet
kisses and bear hugs. Be specific about what
you're proud about. "Dad, I'm really proud of
the way you treat Mom so nice. Some of my
friends don't have parents like that."

❧ "I need your advice." Even if you don't need
their advice, ask for it. If they give it to you,
listen attentively, take notes, and thank them
for their wisdom and valuable insights.
Parents love knowing you need them for more
than their money and the keys to the car. And
hey, you might just get some good advice to go
with the good feelings you generate.

LEARN THE FINE ART OF NEGOTIATION

Part of growing up is learning how to negotiate. This life skill will
serve you well not only with your parents but with just about
everybody else you deal with in the future, like bosses, car sales-
men, teachers, husbands, and wives. Adults negotiate with each
other to solve problems and resolve conflicts. Little kids throw
tantrums. If you check the mirror, you'll notice you're not a little
kid anymore. It's time to learn the fine art of negotiation.

As a teenager, you can expect conflict with your parents
from time to time. Nobody has to tell you that. You want to do
something, but they say no. Or they want you to do something,

and you don't want to do it. That kind of conflict is normal. So how do you handle it?

Basically, you have two choices. You can either negotiate or be a jerk. You can either try to find a solution that satisfies both you and your parents (a win-win), or you can be stubborn and go the winner-takes-all route, hoping they'll just give up and give in. But if experience is any teacher, you'll not only lose more of these battles than you win, but you'll convince your parents you're still a child. You'll lose freedom—not gain it.

So, the choice should be obvious. It's smart to negotiate whenever you can. There will be times, of course, when it's smart NOT to negotiate. That's when your parents are right and you know darn well that they are. The best thing to do in those situations is to save your breath and obey. You'll actually gain more with obedience than with negotiation. Consider it a nice deposit into your trust fund.

But other times you may be absolutely sure that your parents aren't listening to you or that you're being treated unfairly. You're tempted to argue with them or to disobey, but find a better solution. It's time to negotiate. Here are a few guidelines:

First, figure out why the conflict exists. Maybe your parents have needs that conflict with yours. One example is their need for you to be safe so they won't have to worry. You, on the other hand, have a need to be a teenager, which means taking a few risks and engaging in activities that sometimes have the word *extreme* associated with them. If you can find a way to meet both sets of needs, then a negotiation might work. Maybe you can meet their need for you to be safe by taking extra precautions (wearing a helmet, for example), checking in with them regularly, or agreeing to some kind of adult supervision. Rather than getting into a big fight with one side winning and the other side losing, you get a win-win. This usually requires both sides to compromise a little bit.

Here's another example. Let's say you want to use the car to go to a basketball game. Your dad says no because he needs the car to go to a meeting. Notice that your *needs* have nothing to do with the car. You just want to go to the basketball game. But he wants to go to a meeting. Try to find some way you can work out the transportation so that both needs are met. Don't get sidetracked by an argument over who gets to use the car. If you do that, you'll probably lose and end up staying home. Find out if you can get a ride with someone else, or take your dad to his meeting, and pick him up later. Even if you can't stay for the whole game, it's better than not going at all...right?

Second, be willing to strike a bargain. Sometimes negotiating with your parent is figuring out what you can give up in exchange for what you want. This is done in business all the time. For example, you might offer this: "I'll stay home and watch the kids so you can go out on Saturday night, if you'll let me go out on Friday night." Or, "I'll spend an hour a day reading, if you'll agree to forget summer school." Don't lose everything because you're not willing to give up something in exchange.

Bargains like this, by the way, have to be made in good faith. If you offer something in a bargain, you must deliver on your end of the bargain. Don't make the offer if you don't plan to follow through. If your parents agree to forget summer school, don't blow off the daily hour of reading and assume your folks will just forget about it. This is not a bargain, it's a con job, and it will backfire on you.

Third, be willing to suggest a trial period. Sometimes parents won't allow you to do something because they fear what *might* happen. Let's say you ask to take an after-school job and they say, *"No, because your grades will suffer."* Don't get into a big argument over whether they will or won't suffer. Instead, suggest a trial period. You can say, *"Would you be open to letting me get a job for just one month? If my grades go down, I'll give it up. But if they don't, then I get another month. We can reevaluate each month, and if my grades go down because of my job, I'll quit."* Again, this kind of bargain must be made in good faith. Be willing to give up the job if your grades tank.

Fourth, know when to give up on lost causes. A time will come when you're negotiating as skillfully as you possibly can and then, without warning, your parents will make a really good point. They're right, you're wrong, and you know it. Now what are you going to do? Well, you can keep insisting, like a dummy, that you are right, but this rarely works. You'll end up not only losing, but looking really stupid. It's best to just say, *"You know, you're absolutely right. I didn't think of that."* Admit defeat, and save your negotiating skills for another day.

Fifth, don't try to change your parents. You can negotiate with your parents, but you shouldn't try to change them. Let's say you want to get a tattoo. But your parents have a strong belief that tattoos are graffiti on the temple of God and therefore morally wrong. In this case, you probably aren't going to get a tattoo unless you disobey them, which you don't want to do. In some areas you have to accept that they aren't going to change. Save your negotiating for issues that don't require them to give up their beliefs, their values, their personalities, or even their neuroses.

> *I just found out that I got an F in English. I told my mom, and she took it pretty well and didn't yell or anything. I figured it would be better if she heard it from me instead of finding out later by reading my report card.*
> —Tomas, age 16

HEAD 'EM OFF AT THE PASS - - - - - -

Here's a free idea you can thank me for later. Next time you blow it and do something really dumb, don't wait around for your parents to finally discover your lapse in judgment and then chew you out royally for it. Instead, head 'em off at the pass!

In case you're not familiar with this strategy, watch some old cowboy movies. Usually the good guys on their white horses always manage to get out in front of the bad guys and ambush them at the pass. I don't think any *actual* cowboys ever did this, but in the movies, it always worked.

And it can work for you. It's a lot easier to tell your parents,

"*Boy, did I ever blow it!*" than to hear them say to you, "*How could you be so stupid?*" What you want to do is beat them to the pass and own up to your mistake. They will probably be so caught off guard by your admission of guilt and repentant attitude that they'll cut you some slack and be a lot more lenient. If you try to cover up your crime, however, you'll probably not only be punished for your misdeed, but also for obstruction of justice.

Let's say your parents repeatedly warned you about making expensive long-distance calls on the house phone. But you weren't thinking about that when you returned Horatio's phone call at the number he left on the answering machine. He said he was having problems with his parents, and knew you were reading a great book on the subject. He needed your help, so you called him back. After sharing your vast knowledge with Horatio for two hours, you found out that he wasn't home like you thought he was. He was on a trip with his parents in New York City! Uh-oh. Cha-ching!

Now, if you just shut up about it and wait for your parents to get the phone bill, you will not only get the lecture and some harsh new telephone rules, but you will also get $34.50 in phone charges deducted from your allowance. But...if you head 'em off at the pass and tell them what happened before they discover it on their own...there's a chance you'll only get a short version of the lecture, and maybe they'll decide to absorb the extra expense and write it off to a good learning experience for you. It may not work out exactly like that, but you can be sure that things are always worse when you try to conceal your screw-ups.

Keep in mind that this strategy can only be used once per screw-up. All bets are off the second time around.

YOU MAKE THE CALL – – – – – – – – – –

Along the same lines, remember that parents are always impressed when their kids show enough thoughtfulness and responsibility to call and let them know what they're up to. I've heard parents brag to each other, *"My kid is really good about calling and letting us know when he'll be home. Is yours?"* The buttons will just about pop off their shirts.

Remember what we said about parents earlier. They are chronic worrywarts; and when they don't know what you're doing, or when you turn up late, they naturally assume you're in the worst kind of danger. They expect to turn on the late news and see your mutilated body being hauled off to the county morgue. You've been raped, run over, kidnapped, murdered, mugged, or drugged. You've been taken hostage by terrorists. It doesn't have to be possible; it just has to be bad. By the time you get home, your parents will be so concerned about you and moved with compassion that they'll be ready to kill you.

You can avoid all this by making one simple phone call. Even if you messed up—*especially* if you messed up—make the call. It's far better to say, *"Dad, I blew it. I let the time totally get away from me. I'm a jerk. I made you worry, and I'm sorry. I'll be home in half an hour,"* than to try to sneak in the back door pretending nothing happened. At least you'll eliminate a half hour that your parents might spend plotting your execution. Put that cell phone they bought for you to good use. Put your parents on speed dial #1.

GET THINGS CLEAR – – – – – – – – – –

Many problems you have with your parents stem from misunderstandings and wrong assumptions. Is it that you have to be *home* by midnight or *leave the party* by midnight? Did they say you could have *one friend* over or *a whole bunch of friends*? Did they say you could use the car *to go to the mall only* or *to go anywhere within the continental United States?* Don't assume. Get things clear.

I know sometimes you'd rather just leave well enough alone. A nice thick fog leaves you all kinds of room to misinterpret what your parents said, but why set yourself up for more conflict and scolding? While you may see some short-term benefits in allowing an unclear situation to exist, one long-term consequence will most certainly be that your parents will no longer trust your judgment. Do your parents and yourself a favor; make sure you understand their expectations exactly. And let them know in advance exactly what you're going to do. Get rid of the fog. Clear things up. If you discuss these things in advance, you'll probably get a better deal than you expect. Then everybody wins.

> *My mother and I are getting along better since I started talking to her about everything.*
> —Michelle, age 17

- - - - SHARE YOUR LIFE WITH THEM

I know, you're thinking they know too much already. Besides, if you tell them stuff they'll just use it against you, or butt in and criticize, or get mad. Okay, that's a possibility. But you don't have to tell them anything you don't want to. Skip telling them about that unscheduled trip you made today to the principal's office. Don't clue them in on your big plans to drop out of school and become a professional transient. Just crack the door a little bit, and give them a glimpse into the life of a real teenager like yourself. Take the initiative to break the silence, and share some of your life with your parents. Open up the communication lines.

And why, pray tell, would you ever want to do anything like that? Because you will never understand your parents, and they will never understand you, unless you talk to each other. You simply must learn how to communicate with them on some level. Start with small talk if nothing else (*Hey dad, how 'bout them Chargers*) but as you go deeper, you'll find your relationship with them will get a whole lot better. And yes, you get a payoff. The more they know you and know about your needs, the better position they'll be in to meet your needs. They might even get some ideas for their Christmas shopping list. So talk to them already!

Here are a few talk tips.

👀 *Answer their questions with actual answers.* Pretend your parents really are interested in the answer when they ask, "How was school?" or "What are you going to do today?" Don't automatically assume they're prying into your private life or trying to gather evidence they can use against you. They know you aren't dumb enough to tell them everything anyway. Give them the benefit of the doubt and assume that, at the very least, they're looking for a little conversation. Throw them some crumbs. Instead of saying, "Nuthin'" or "I dunno," give them a little bit of information. *"We saw a cool video about the Battle of Gettysburg in our U.S. History class."* Things will start rolling from there. You don't have to mention that you slept through your English class or blew up the chemistry lab. But say something that sounds like a real answer.

👀 *Make the first move if they don't.* Sometimes parents don't talk for the same reasons you don't. They don't want conflict. Or they don't want to sound stupid. Or they don't know what to say or just don't think conversation is necessary. So, be the adult if they aren't taking the lead. Just say something like *"Hey, Dad, did I tell you about the conversation I had with Coach Johnson yesterday?"* or *"Mom, when you get a few minutes, I'll update you on some of the latest gossip from school."* Surprise your parents with an invitation to talk, and you'll be surprised by how good it feels to be an adult.

👀 *Don't be afraid to let them get inside your head.* As you become more comfortable having conversations with your parents, risk going a little deeper. *"You know, Dad,*

I've been thinking..." Or, "Mom, have you ever felt like..."
Good relationships are all about meeting another
person's needs, and the idea here is to give your parents a fast track to your needs. The more they
understand how you feel and what your needs are,
they better they will be able to respond appropriately
and not overreact. If they know you're feeling over-
whelmed by that algebra course, they won't get nearly as upset when you tell them you're getting a D in it.

TAKE AN INTEREST IN THEIR BORING LIVES TOO

It's hard to find much that's very interesting about being a parent,
it's true. But work with me here. Finding out more about your
parents has real value—and the best place to get that information is directly from the horse's mouth. Think of it as doing a little intelligence gathering.

If you're afraid you'll fall asleep listening to them talk about
their lives right now, ask them questions about their preadult
days. So far, all you've heard are the rumors. You heard your
mom really wanted to be an actress. You heard your dad got cut
from his high school football team when his shoe fell off trying to
kick a field goal. But you've never actually heard them talk about
any of this stuff...to you, anyway.

If nothing else, you can use this information to your advantage later. "But Dad, you had a car when you were sixteen," or—
next time you get in trouble—"Well, I guess I'm just a chip off the
old block, huh?" One big plus is that they'll be forced to remember
a little more of what their teen years were like and see you as
more of an equal. They may begin to cut you a little more slack
when you remind them of the raunchy stuff they listened to on
the radio when they were your age or how poorly they did in
world history class.

Icebreaker Questions
1. Where did you grow up? In the city? On a farm?

Overseas?

2. What kind of relationship did you have with your parents? Brothers and sisters?

3. Were you rich? Poor? In-between? What did your parents do for a living?

4. Who were your best friends in high school? Do you still keep in touch?

5. What were your toughest classes in school?

6. What did you do for fun? What about parties? Did you ever get into any kind of trouble?

7. Did you attend church as a teenager? Where? Did you have a youth group? What was your relationship with God like?

8. What were the defining world events when you were a kid? What was your September 11th?

9. Did you have a job as a teenager? How old were you when you left home?

10. How did you and mom (or dad) meet? How long did you date before getting married? What was your wedding like?

11. Was sex as big a deal then as it is now? Did you feel pressure to have sex? How did you handle it?

(You'll want to be sure your parents are mature enough to handle topics like these, but they've probably wanted to discuss them with you anyway.)

You can think of other things to talk about, too. And, you don't have to cover all these subjects in one sitting. Take your time, and let your parents know you really are interested in learning more about them and from them. The more you know about your parents, the better window you'll have into their lives, and you'll have more insight into why they act the way they do. Early life experiences shape all of our lives later on. If your parents were poor, that might explain why they're so uptight about money today. If they were wild as teenagers, that might explain why they want to protect you from getting into the same kind of trouble they did, or why they have a hard time setting limits for you.

Then find out about their lives right now. They may not tell you too much because they aren't sure you're interested, or they may not want to bother or worry you. But let them know that you can handle it. It never hurts to ask, *"How was your day, Mom?"* If she gives you an "okay" or a "same old, same old" be patient and keep trying. Maybe you need to be a little more specific. *"You seem a little tired tonight, Dad. Tough day at work?"* or *"Hey Mom, when you get a chance, I'd like to find out how your staff meeting went today."* If you take an interest in their lives and open up the communication lines, you can be sure they'll start treating you differently, and they'll probably let you take down that Winnie the Pooh wallpaper in your bedroom!

– – – – – – – – – WRITE 'EM A NOTE

If you have problems getting your parents' attention or communicating, write them a letter and express how you feel. If you have problems that you want to discuss with them, start the letter by telling them that you are writing because you love them and want to have a better relationship with them. It's just easier for you to write down your feelings than to express them verbally. You can hand the letter to them personally and ask them to read it when they have time, or you can leave it where they will find it, or even mail it to them. If your parents are online, use e-mail.

– – – – – – – – – – –LISTEN UP!

While we're on the subject of communication, let me give you a quick lesson on listening. Obviously, without someone there to listen, it doesn't do much good for anybody to talk. For whatever reason, family members often don't listen to each other very well, and this ruins good communication.

I know it's tough to listen to your parents because they often have a way of talking down to you. It feels as if they're lecturing or nagging. But parents usually do this out of habit. If you stare at the floor or look off into space or stick your fingers in your ears, they pick up right away that you aren't listening; and this forces them to just talk louder. Pretty soon they're yelling. Of course, they don't consider it yelling. Tell them to stop yelling, and they'll say, *"I'M NOT YELLING!!"* They are not lying. They're just trying to get something to stick between your ears.

Listening is the language of love. It really is. That's why God gave us two ears and only one mouth. The best way to let your parents know you love them and want to have a good relationship with them is to become a better listener.

Here's something that might help. Remember the word FAD. When your mom and dad start talking to you, think "Okay, it's time for that listening FAD." F-A-D stands for three important listening steps:

1. Focus
2. Accept
3. Draw out

To *focus*, you give the speaker your undivided attention. If you're sitting at the computer playing video games, hit the pause button and let your screen saver take over while you turn your head and body in your parents' direction and look directly into their eyes while they talk. This may shock your parents so much they'll become speechless.

Then, *accept*. Rather than holding your breath and turning blue, lean forward, raise your eyebrows, nod your head up and down vigorously, and put something other than a look of severe constipation on your face. This is called body language. People really feel uncomfortable if your body language says, *"Why in the world are you wasting my time with this useless drivel. Here's a quarter—call someone who cares."*

Third, *draw out* by asking questions. Even if you don't, pretend you want to hear more. This is sometimes called active listening. You say things like, *"Wow, that's really interesting. And then what happened?"* or *"So what you're saying is that you really think I'm spending too much time on the computer? How much more time can I use it today?"* You may not get a satisfactory answer, but your parents will at least know that you got the message, and they won't have to yell at you. Plus, they may be so blown away by your positive attitude that they catch themselves saying, *"Oh, well, I guess it wouldn't hurt for you to go ahead and finish whatever it is you're doing."*

If you listen to your parents better, I guarantee they'll pick up on that and start listening to you better too.

TAKE TIME TO HANG WITH THEM

Yeah, I know. On the surface this sounds about as exciting as watching grass grow, but work with me here. One of the reasons so many kids have a bad relationship with their parents is they just don't spend enough time with them. Actually this is true for anybody. If you don't spend time with your friends, you'll never be close. If your dad doesn't spend some time with your mom, they won't be close (so let them go away for the weekend and be romantic once in a while, okay?) That's why you want to spend so much time with your boyfriend or girlfriend, right? In fact, you want to be with them ALL THE TIME.

Well, you can't really have a good relationship with your parents if you don't spend some time with them, and I recommend that you find some fun ways to do that.

> *I like to rent movies and have a night in with my mom. And I like to play beach volleyball with my dad.*
> —Sarah, age 16

Derrick, who was 15, told me he had a terrible relationship with his dad until they went on a backpack trip together. His dad suggested hike the Grand Canyon in Arizona together. Derrick really didn't want to go, but his dad finally talked him into it. It was like mountain climbing in reverse. They went down one side of the canyon and up the other, camping out along the way, sleeping in a little tent, and cooking their meals over little campfires. They were out on the trail for a week and experienced bad weather, wind, sunburn, a plague of mosquitoes, and a near-drowning in the Colorado

River, but they had great week together. Derrick said, *"Now my dad and I are really close. He's really cool, and we like to be together."* Wow! Relationships don't usually change that quickly, but maybe it was the kind of quality time they spent together that week. Maybe it was because they had never done anything like that before.

If your mom or dad doesn't suggest something, why don't you? It doesn't have to be a hike in the Grand Canyon. Maybe you could go fishing or play games or go shopping or out to dinner and a movie. Some kids actually ask their parents out on a date and pay for everything themselves. Don't gag on this. Really, it can be fun!

What could you and your parents do together that you would both enjoy? Do you have any hobbies that you'd like to try? How about photography? Music? Computers? Cars? Scrapbooking? Sports? You probably like to do all kinds of things your parents like to do too. Why not do them together once in a while?

> *I love both my parents. But my mom and I get along better. I love my dad, but he annoys me a lot.*
> —Meredith, age 15

Maybe you could ask your parents if you could help plan your next family vacation so that they don't feel like they're dragging you along on theirs. Find out what the budget is and get creative. Whether it's a camping trip, a cruise to the Bahamas, a stay at a downtown hotel, or an African safari, you can use that time to get to know your parents better. Don't hide from them at the amusement park with your friends or siblings. Hang with Mom or Dad, and use that time to have fun, talk, and learn more about them. You don't have to do this *too* often, but even once a year can be a great way to keep things cool between you and your parents.

LEARN TO FORGIVE – – – – – – – – – –

If you have a tough time with some of these ideas because you're totally ticked at your parents, you may need to learn how to forgive them. Maybe you need to just forgive them for being...parents! "Father, forgive them for they know not what they are doing!" (Luke 23:43) Or maybe you have more specific things. Forgive them for treating you like a child even though you're doing your best to show them you're not. Forgive them for putting their needs ahead of yours all the time. Forgive them for not letting you go to that concert with your friends. Forgive them for...well, the list could go on and on, couldn't it?

Look, forgiveness ain't easy. It's making a decision to not allow what someone else did to you ruin your life. If you hang on to your anger and hurt, it may feel good for a little while, and it may work as some kind of retaliation against the one who hurt you, but in the end, it will definitely keep you from being happy. Why let someone else control you like that? You can let go of it and get on with your life. Learn to forgive. Even if the other person doesn't care or even know she's been forgiven, it's a way of cleaning up your own emotional house. Just sweep up all the bad, hateful feelings that clutter up your life, and toss them in the dumpster.

I know, you don't want to forgive someone if they aren't SORRY for what they did to you. You want them to get down on their hands and knees and beg for forgiveness and do something to show that they really mean it, like admit they were wrong and you were right, and then make everything better by paying damages and promising to never do it again. Well, that's not forgiveness, that's a lawsuit.

Forgiveness isn't really about them, anyway. It's about you. What kind of person do you want to be? You can be a selfish, unhappy, and revengeful person who always tries to get even, or you can be a gracious, happy, and forgiving person who always tries to get the most out of life. Who would you rather have for a friend?

Remember, when you forgive people, you aren't setting *them* free from what they've done; you're setting *yourself* free. You can't do that for anyone else; you can only do it for yourself. If you let what someone else has done ruin your life, then they've won. You don't want that to happen.

If you've hung on to your anger for a while, you may not be able to immediately run up and hug your parents and tell them that everything's okay. Forgiveness doesn't always change everything overnight. Anger is like a drug. It sometimes takes a while for you to come down off of it. Forgive them in your heart first. Just make the decision to forgive and forget. Pray that God will help you let it go, and then get on with your life. Once the healing begins (and it will), you can continue to work on the relationship you want to have with them.

Forgiveness is possible even when parents do horrible things to you or your family. I've known young people who forgave their parents for abusing them, abandoning them, even trying to kill them. More often than not, forgiveness like that has a powerful effect on people. In the Bible, while Stephen was being killed for his faith in Christ (Acts 7), he forgave those who were killing him. One of those people, Saul, later became Paul, the apostle who wrote much of the New Testament. And of course, when Jesus forgave those who were killing him (Luke 23:34), he changed the whole world.

It's okay to be angry with your parents, but don't let it prevent you from doing what's right. Let it go as soon as you can. Remember what the Bible says: "Be kind and compassionate to one another, forgiving each other, just as in Christ God forgave you" (Ephesians 4:32).

STAY PLUGGED IN

By now you may be thinking to yourself, *"Yeah, right. Who does this guy think I am, anyway, Billy Graham? Mother Teresa? There's no way I can do all this stuff."*

I know it seems like a tall order. But you don't have to do it all. Just do some of it. Doing something always beats doing nothing at all. More often that not, it turns out to be all that's needed.

Remember the kid in the Bible who offered to share his lunch with 5,000 people? Everybody laughed at him. But Jesus took the boy's lunch, thanked him for it, and started feeding everyone. They even had food left over. All Jesus needed was a little something to work with, and he did the rest. In the same way, you may get laughed at for doing some of the things I've suggested in this chapter. But do them anyway, and let God do the rest. He'll make your *something* into *something big.*

> **My relationship with my parents is really important to me. I'm so blessed to have such wonderful role models that have taught me good morals.**
> —Sarah, age 16

But you'll need to stay plugged in to the power source. Your power comes from God, through Jesus Christ. Paul wrote, "I can do everything through him who gives me strength (Philippians 4:13)." He wasn't just blowing smoke. When God inspires you to do something, he also gives you the power to pull it off. But you need to stay close to him.

Read your Bible daily. Get involved in a church youth group. Discover how cool it is to worship with other Christians. Pray for your parents every day. And ask God to provide you with wisdom and courage to honor your parents every day by doing the right thing. Stay plugged in. Need a power verse? This is 220-volt power (Galatians 2:20): "I have been crucified with Christ and I no longer live, but Christ lives in me. The life I live in the body, I live by faith in the Son of God, who loved me and gave himself for me."

REMEMBER THE LAW
OF THE FARM - - - - - - - - - - -

I want to mention one more thing as we come to the end of this chapter. Be patient—both with yourself and your parents. Even if you put every one of these ideas into practice right away, you may not see change for a long time—maybe a year or more. But don't give up.

I remember talking with a girl named Jenny who tried a random act of kindness on her mom. But instead of making her mother happy, she only made her more suspicious. *"Okay, what are you up to now? What are you trying to get out of me?"* Jenny was so upset by her mom's response that she decided not to do anything nice for her mother ever again.

But sometimes you don't get what you want right away. Author Stephen Covey talks about a principle worth remembering, called "the law of the farm." I'm not a farmer, but I do try to grow a small vegetable garden behind my house every year. I've learned that to get delicious homegrown tomatoes, corn, peas, zucchini, and string beans, I must do certain things. First, I must prepare the soil by turning it with a rototiller. I also add nutrients like compost and fertilizer. Then, usually in late March or April, I plant the seeds. After weeks and sometimes months of daily watering and cultivating, i finally get a harvest. Our poor kids have to eat peas and zucchini for dinner every night.

Now I have to admit that some years I planted my garden and then like a dummy forgot to take care of it. I didn't water it properly. I let insects or gophers take over. As you might guess, we didn't get much of a harvest those years. Dead tomato plants don't produce too many tomatoes.

That's the law of the farm. Most of the good things in life require time, effort, and adherence to the laws of nature. You can't speed up the process, take shortcuts, or cheat the system. And you don't want to give up if you don't get results right away. You have to do the right thing, then wait, which is not a popular concept in today's world of fast cars, fast food, and fast everything else.

So hang in there. You've got time on your side. Don't forget that your teen years are like riding the whitewater rapids on a river. Things can get pretty bumpy. But it's a long river; and if you can keep from falling out of the boat, you'll come to smooth water up ahead. So be patient. Put some of these ideas to work, and give them time. You'll reap a harvest that will bless your family for a long time to come.

BUT YOU DON'T KNOW MY PARENTS

DAD Mom

(EXTRA HELP FOR XTRA-TOUGH PROBLEMS)

This chapter has extra help for kids who face unique challenges with their parents. Maybe that's you. But keep in mind that the first four chapters of this book apply to *everybody*, so be sure to read them first. You may think, *"But my parents aren't like other parents!"* Well, join the club. All parents are different, and every family is unique.

Don't blow off the ideas in the first four chapters just because you think your parents are a little weird. I didn't write them for normal parents or normal families. I wrote them for all teenagers who want to have a better relationship with their parents—regardless of their parents' marital status, ages, personalities, occupations, or anything else. You may need to be flexible, selective, or creative in applying everything in this book, but that's why God gave you all that gray matter between your ears. You can figure it out!

Still, you may face some special problems at home that have you stumped. You aren't sure what to do. Quite frankly, you may not find the answers in this book or any book. If that's the case, don't stop looking for help. You may need to talk to someone who can help you, like a pastor, a youth minister, a school counselor, or a grandparent. You may need to do that regardless. You can be sure that *someone* out there *can* help you, and you should take the initiative to get the help you need. If you've read this far, I have a hunch you'll do exactly that.

"MY PARENTS AREN'T AROUND VERY MUCH" – – – – – – – – – – –

Maybe your parents are so busy or so uninvolved in your life that you feel as if you're practically raising yourself. Now some teenagers might think that's a pretty cool arrangement. No parents around? So who's complaining? Of course, if that's your situation, you know it's not quite all it's cracked up to be. You may feel lonely or unloved or find yourself forced into dealing with a lot of extra pressure that really gets you down. Maybe your mom or dad has to work long hours to make ends meet, or they travel a lot, or they just have too much going on in their lives.

Your parents may not realize the impact this has on you. Talk to them about it. Find a time and a place when you can sit down, and let them know how you feel. Don't criticize them or try to make them feel more guilty than they already feel; but let them know you would like

things to be different. Let them know you really want to have a good relationship with them and that their involvement in your life is important to you right now. Your honesty may help them decide to make some changes in their lives and adjust some of their priorities. Chances are they just let the busyness of their lives crowd out some of the more important things.

Meanwhile, don't give up on them. Don't crowd your own life with activities that take you away from your parents. Spend as much time with them as you can. Even a little time with them beats no time at all. Remember that you'll leave home sooner than you think, and your opportunities to be close to your parents may be gone forever.

"MY PARENTS DON'T CARE WHAT I DO"

Then that leaves you. You'll have to do all the caring.

It's too bad some parents don't care enough to give their kids the guidance they need or have the guts to set limits for them. Parents who allow their kids (even encourage them) to do whatever they want—including things that are immoral or illegal—are, quite frankly, irresponsible parents. Some kids might think they're *perfect* parents, but if they're yours, you know you're missing out on something very important in life.

But remember: it's your life, not theirs—and you are just as irresponsible as they are if you don't care either. Plenty of kids today can get away with anything, and so they do. They head off to Cancun on spring break and get totally wasted for a week while their parents stay home and pick up the tab. Many of these kids end up being raped, seriously injured, diseased, or killed. They end up losers now and losers later. Is that how you want to live your life? I don't think so.

I have a pretty good relationship with my parents, but more so with my dad. He actually raised me, and my mom left us after the divorce. I see my mom, but my relationship with my dad is deeper than with my mom.

—Susanna, age 13

If you don't think your parents are involved enough in your life, talk to them about it. You may be afraid to lose some of your freedom by bringing up the subject, but maybe they care more than you think. Maybe they care enough to trust you with your freedom, and they expect you to live up, not down, to their expectations of you. Maybe they decided to give you additional freedom because they resented their parents' strictness when they were teenagers. But whatever the reason, you have choices to make, and you may need to make them on your own. Choose wisely.

"MY PARENTS SPLIT UP" – – – – – – –

Divorce is a bad deal for everyone involved. Hardly anything is tougher than having parents who split up. That's why the Bible teaches that divorce is never the best way to solve family problems. Nobody wins. Everybody gets hurt. Of course, if your parents are divorced, you know that already. You know how it feels.

You may wonder what caused your parents' divorce. Why did they have to split up? Whose fault was it? Didn't they take vows to stay married until "death do us part"? Why didn't they do what they said they would do? Why didn't they try to work things out?

You may never know the answers to those questions, but one thing's for sure. Nobody starts out planning to get a divorce. Your parents, like most couples that get married, undoubtedly expected to love and cherish each other for the rest of their lives. They didn't want things to turn out the way they did. But after they were married, they had problems that must have seemed insurmountable to them. Ultimately, they decided that divorce was the best way to solve them. Right or wrong, they believed divorce was best for everybody, including you.

Even though the reasons for a divorce are complicated and often impossible to explain, it's natural to want to blame something or someone for your parents' divorce. You may want to blame yourself. Don't. You were not the cause of their problems. You didn't get divorced, your parents did. You are not responsible for their divorce, nor is it a reflection of anything you did.

But you will feel the impact of it. You may feel betrayed, depressed, confused, or angry, and feel a void of insecurity and loneliness where their marriage used to be. On the other hand you may feel relieved that the conflict and tension is finally over. You may find yourself living in two houses instead of one if your parents have some kind of shared custody arrangement. You may not be able to see one parent or the other except on weekends or even less frequently. You may find yourself caught in a tug-of-war between your parents. All this can hurt and be very disruptive to your life. At least you know you're not alone. Many of your friends have gone through the same thing.

Remember that ultimately you have the choice to make the best of the situation or to let yourself be victimized by it. I know a lot of kids who use their parents' divorce as a convenient excuse to be rebellious or irresponsible. Please don't do that. As we said earlier, you can choose to be either a thermostat or a thermometer. Some things are out of your control (like your parents' divorce), but you DO have control over all kinds of things. You can decide, for example, how you treat your parents. You can decide whether you will allow them to involve you in their disputes. You can decide whether to blame them for your problems or take responsibility for solving them yourself. You decide whether to let your parents' divorce bring you down or let it inspire you to rise above the situation and do better than anyone thinks you can. You have a lot more power than you think. When you change, things around you start to change.

As for those things you can't do anything about, the best approach is to avoid blaming anyone and do all you can to demonstrate God's love in the middle of a tough situation. Try to love and honor both your parents even though they find it impossible to love and honor each other.

"MY PARENTS TRY TO COMMUNICATE THROUGH ME" – – – –

It's tough to be caught in the middle of a divorce or separation. When parents split up, there usually a lot of anger and conflict, and sometimes parents make a mistake and force their kids to become messengers or informants. One parent may want to know what the other is doing, who is he seeing, how much money he has, and so on. One may ask you to deliver a message to the other so that he doesn't have to do it himself. If that's the case, let them know you won't participate in this game. Just say something like *"Mom, you'll have to ask him yourself,"* or *"Dad, I really love both of you and don't want to hurt either one of you by delivering messages back and forth. I'm afraid I'll say the wrong thing."* You may need to set a few boundaries for yourself like those in the sidebar.

Communication Boundaries
- Make sure your parents know you don't want them to bad-mouth the other parent,

– – – – – – – – – – – – – – – –

stepparent, or stepkids in front of you.

- Ask them not to involve you in their money problems. They should be clear and agree on who is responsible to provide money for the things you need.
- When one parent talks bad about the other, ask him to stop, or excuse yourself and walk away.
- Don't tell one parent any negative things the other parent said about her. You'll become part of the problem by making things worse.
- Don't take sides in a dispute. Be loving and loyal to both parents.
- Don't accept bribes for your loyalty. Your relationship with your parents is far more important than money or things.
- Don't deliver messages. If they don't like the message, they may take it out on the messenger.
- Don't be a shoulder to cry on or a counselor for your parents. That's not really your role, and you shouldn't be put in that position.

Let your parents know you care about them both, but protect yourself from being caught in a tug-of-war between them. You may prefer living with or being with one parent over the other, but you shouldn't play one against the other or try to manipulate them for your own gain. It's important for you to keep a good relationship with both your parents regardless of how things turn out after their divorce.

"MY STEPPARENT IS A PAIN TO GET ALONG WITH"

This is a common problem for teenagers in blended families. When your mom or dad's new husband or wife tries to step in and become an instant parent for you, you may have a hard time accepting his or her role in your life. But the stepparent is in a tough spot. Obviously no one can completely replace your absent mom or dad. Your stepparent may feel resentful toward you because you don't consider him or her part of your real family or because you always compare him or her with your mom or dad. They may feel jealous of the special relationship you have with your natural parents. All these things can result in a difficult and awkward situation both for your stepparent and for you.

If that's the case, you may want to talk to your mom or dad about the situation and get some advice. Be specific and talk about any problems you have with your stepparent. If you're willing to find a good solution, you will find it.

Should you obey your stepparent when they tell you what you can or cannot do? The answer is yes. Even though he or she is not your real parent, the Bible's command to obey your parents doesn't make that distinction. You are under your parents' authority, whoever they are and however they got there. This also applies to kids who are adopted or living in foster homes. Unless your parents force you to commit a sin, the right thing to do is to be obedient and respectful of the authority God has given them.

Here's a challenge for you. Next time you're tempted to resist your stepparent's authority, ask yourself, "Would I feel any differently about this if it came from my real parent?" If you're honest, you'll probably discover that you wouldn't. If your real parent were the one nagging about doing your homework before watching TV instead of your stepparent, you'd still be just as annoyed by it. Don't use your stepparent's lame-duck position as an excuse to be disobedient or disrespectful.

But if you genuinely have problems with a power-hungry stepparent, the sidebar tells you some things you can do.

Stepparent Savvy
℘ Ask your parent if he or she could be the one to make and enforce rules until your relationship with your stepparent improves.
℘ Let your stepparent know you would like to have a

better relationship with him or her, and take
steps to improve it.

& Ask your parent what to do. Listen and get some
advice, then do what he or she tells you to do.

Don't automatically label your stepparent as wicked and evil. Where that stereotype came from, I'll never know. They need your help. It ain't easy to step into a family-in-progress and try to help raise kids who automatically think you exist just to make their lives miserable. Do what you can to build a good relationship with them just as you would with your real parents, and watch what happens. Your life will get a whole lot better (not to mention theirs).

Remember that Jesus honored and obeyed *both* of his parents...and Joseph was his stepparent (Luke 2:51).

"MY PARENTS ARE – – – – – – –ALWAYS IN A BAD MOOD"

Even if your parents are in a bad mood just some of the time, it can feel like always.

Lots of things can affected a person's mood. If by bad mood you mean quiet and withdrawn (rather than mean and angry), it could just be a personality trait. Some people are not very outgoing or they lack a sense of humor. They are more serious-natured and that's just the way they're wired. They can't help it. With time, you'll learn how to adjust to your mom or dad's personality and interpret their moods accordingly. I know some people who (until you get to know them) always appear unhappy. But they aren't unhappy at all. They are just introverted and quiet by nature. There's nothing wrong with them.

You may wish your parents were more fun loving and full of laughter, but be patient and understanding with them. Try not to compare your parents with your friends' happy-go-lucky parents who always play practical jokes and do fun things with their kids. Accept your parents as they are, and learn to play to their strengths, not their weaknesses.

Maybe their bad mood is a reaction to something going on in their lives right now. Assuming that *you* are not the problem, they may have problems that you don't know about. Go back and read about some of the problems parents face in Chapter Two. Job stress, money problems, marriage problems, PMS, menopause, clinical depression—the list goes on and on. Most of these are temporary, and your parents probably just need a little time to get over them. If your dad comes home from work with a frown on his face and plops down in the easy chair mumbling things to himself, it may not be the best time to ask for a raise in your allowance. He may just need a little mini-vacation—some time to rest, recover his senses, and get back to normal.

When you detect negative signals from your parents, try not to over-react with negative responses of your own. Be as positive as you can, and avoid being just another source of irritation to them. As a teenager, you know how bad feelings can come and go. What matters is what we do with them.

"MY PARENTS EXPECT ME TO BE SOMETHING I'M NOT" - - - -

Almost all parents have great expectations for their children, and almost no child ever lives up to them. I'm not talking about those *"We expect you to be home at ten o'clock"* or *"We expect you to go with us to your sister's piano recital"* expectations. No, I'm talking about the ones that have nothing to do with anything you can control. In their heads parents usually have a picture of their Ideal Child, the one they believe would make them the proudest parents on the planet. Sometimes parents envision their children becoming what they themselves could never be. Their expectations are not very realistic.

Of course, you probably have unrealistic expectations of your parents as well. Maybe you wish they were different in some way—more stylish, more successful, better looking, or more fun to be around. Everybody has unrealistic expectations of each other at times.

So what do you do if your parents want you to be something

you're not? Maybe they want you to be an all-American, preppie, premed student. But you lean more toward becoming a drummer in a grunge band. Should you try to be something you really don't want to be?

First, remember that your parents are trying to guide you toward success in life, and they may have a better idea about how to get there than you do. If part of their "wanting you to be something you're not" includes getting your education, doing your homework, and being responsible as a student, then they're right. Your most important task—besides helping to create a healthy family at home—is to learn as much as you can about the world and about yourself. Being a good student is an important part of the process; and your education will help you, even if you ultimately decide to pursue your dream of being a rock star.

But if your parents chose a specific career for you, they may be making a big mistake. If you have no desire to become a brain surgeon, you're not going to be a very good one even if you have the proper education. But don't rebel against your parents' plan for you just to prove them wrong. If they want you to become a doctor, for example, they may believe you have the aptitude and skills to be a good one. Give it a try at least, and see where it leads.

I know a young lady named Alison whose parents encouraged her to pursue a career in law and the financial industry. Alison, however, wanted to be a professional musician. She decided to follow her parents' advice, and she graduated with a degree in finance from Harvard University. After graduation, she got a job working at a major Wall Street firm, but she never gave up her dream of playing music professionally. Today, she lives in Nashville and is a successful performer and recording artist. But her education in law and finance came in real handy. She not only is a successful musician, but she started her own record company. Read her story at www.alisonbrown.com.

Sometimes parents want their sons or daughters to fulfill dreams they weren't able to accomplish themselves; sometimes they just want them to follow in their footsteps. You, on the other hand, need to consider all the possibilities that lie before you.

What are you good at? What do you want to be doing 10 or 20 years from now? What can you do today to prepare yourself for your future? If you're certain your goals are in conflict with the goals your parents have set for you, you need to talk with them about it. Let them know you have no desire or intention of pursuing the career they chose for you.

Likewise, if your parents push you to be something right now that you can't be, tell them how you feel. They may want you to be a cheerleader, a football star, a beauty queen, or a leader in the church youth group, and they pressure you to pursue these things. You may choose to please your parents by doing the best you can, but if you are certain you can't succeed at these things, be honest with them and help them understand you better. With time, they'll change their expectations of you and learn to accept you just the way you are.

"MY PARENTS ARE TOO STRICT" - - -

Chances are pretty good that your parents aren't any stricter than other parents. It may appear that some of your friends get a lot more freedom than you do, but your friends probably think their parents are way more strict than yours. It's all a matter of perspective.

Actually, if you didn't think your parents were strict, there would probably be something wrong with you. That's because you are becoming an adult. The defining characteristic of adulthood is freedom from parental authority. It's natural for you to want more freedom as you get older, and the challenge of being a parent is to find that middle ground of where to give you more freedom, but still be parents. As long as you're at home, you'll always have *some* rules. It's their house.

Anyway, you wouldn't want parents who weren't somewhat strict. Think about it. What if your parents said to you, *"Hey, go ahead and do whatever you want. I really don't care if you drink or smoke or do drugs or drive recklessly or even come home at night."* While that may sound like a pretty cool deal at first, it wouldn't take long for you to realize you have the worst kind of parents. The message would be clear. *"We don't love you. We don't have time for you. You are unimportant."* Sometimes it helps to remember that your parents' rules usually represent how much they care about you.

But you say your parents are super-strict—beyond caring to total domination? Well, unless you have a parent named Attila the Hun, you probably just have controlling, perfectionist parents who have a tough time accepting the fact that you're growing up. Some parents are more afraid to let go of the rope than others. They're scared to death you'll hang yourself.

This may not be their fault or even yours. It's just the way they are. If you've given them reasons to worry about you more, then you can expect more rules. But if you haven't, maybe your parents are just incurable control freaks. It's in their genetic makeup. They are micromanagers who love details. They like to be in charge, and they feel very uneasy when they aren't.

If that describes your parents, there's a better way to respond than with total rebellion. The best thing you can do is to continue to prove to your folks that you can handle more freedom and more responsibility than they think. And you don't do that by arguing or shouting. Actions speak louder than words. Be a responsible person, and they will likely give you more freedom. And if that doesn't work, talk to them about it. Let them know how you feel. Most parents really do want to help their kids become all that God created them to be.

Parents can be unreasonable at times, but so can you. Remember that the more slack you cut your parents and the more you forgive them for not being perfect, the more they will do the same for you.

"MY PARENTS PUSH GOD ON ME TOO MUCH"

If your parents have a strong faith in God, they probably do everything they can to make sure you grow up to have faith in God too. The Bible commands them to do whatever it takes to pass their faith along to you (Deuteronomy 6), and if they don't do that, they're being unfaithful to God and to their religion. For this reason you need to be understanding and grateful you have such good parents. Not too many parents today care enough about their kids to drag them to church every week and put up with all the grief the kids give them about it.

Does that mean you have to be as religious as they are? No, it doesn't. They can't force you to believe anything you don't want to believe. But they may insist you go to church or participate with them in family devotions or other religious activities. As long as you live under your parents' roof, you are obliged to obey. As the old saying goes, "You can lead a horse to water, but you can't make him drink."

Remember, faith is very important to those who have it. They want others to have it too. That's why it may seem like your parents push God on you. If they make you uncomfortable or cause you to be resentful toward God or them, their efforts may be backfiring. Talk to them about it. Let them know how you feel. You might say something like *"Right now I just need some space to find God on my own."* They may still insist on church attendance, but they may give you more freedom to explore your faith on your own. Whatever you do, keep searching for the kind of spirituality that will be meaningful for you. Your parents won't give up on you and neither will God.

"MY PARENTS ARE NOT CHRISTIANS, BUT I AM" – – – – – –

You have a great opportunity to share your faith with your parents while you're still at home. It would be a very cool thing if your parents became Christians because of you. It's has happened before! I personally know parents who came to church because their kids convinced them they needed to know Christ and to find what the kids found.

The first thing to remember is that your *life*, not preaching, is the best way to communicate your faith to your parents. St. Francis of Assisi once said, "Preach the Gospel at all times. If necessary, use words." He meant that words only add to what people can see by our actions. What we do communicates a lot more than what we say.

That doesn't mean you have to be the perfect kid...with a clean bedroom...straight As...all your chores done without griping, etc. It just means that you're growing in your faith and trying to live the best Christian life you can. If your parents notice the changes in your life—even the small ones—they may be attracted to the Jesus you know.

Don't preach at your parents, but let them know you're serious about your faith. If you have the opportunity, don't be afraid to tell them what you believe and explain the gospel to them as you understand it. Invite your parents to go to church with you if they don't already attend. Or you might consider inviting them to a Christian concert or to help chaperone a youth group activity. But don't worry if your parents don't respond right away. They may have some religious baggage or other issues that keep them away from the church. Just keep praying for them and living at home the way you think Christ would want you to.

What if your parents have a problem with your being a Christian? Talk to them about it. Let them know in a respectful way that you're old enough to choose your own spiritual path. Let them know you aren't judging them or trying to act superior to them. You just have a new relationship with God that is very meaningful to you. And don't get discouraged if your parents get on your case for being a Christian or bring it up when you blow it. *"Oh, so that's how Christians act, huh? They talk back to their parents and pick on their little sisters!"*

If your faith in Christ causes problems at home, find out what they are. You may need to be careful not to let your church activities interfere with your family life. You may need to avoid trying to convert other family members. You will definitely want to set a good example and honor and obey your parents unless they require you to deny your faith in Jesus. Jesus told his disciples to expect persecution, even from family members (Matthew 10:21). But he also said, "Pray for those who persecute you." (Matthew 5:44)

"MY PARENTS ARE IMMIGRANTS FROM A DIFFERENT CULTURE" - - - -

This is a common problem for teenagers who have parents from another country with different customs and values. It can cause a real clash of cultures. If you have immigrant parents, they may want to bring you up the same way they were brought up, and you can't blame them. Their traditions are very important to them. But you have to grow up in a different world, with different traditions, and different standards. What can you do?

You can become a bridge between the old world and the new. You've planted your feet firmly in the new world and are adapting to new friends, new standards of living, and new influences that your parents never had. Be patient with them. They're doing the best they can, but they're frightened and cling to what is familiar. You don't want to be their enemy, but their educator. You can help them understand the new world and the things you learn and experience.

Remember that your parents had a lifetime of learning a different way of life. Now they're in a strange world, and they aren't sure what to do. They may feel cut off from their roots and from the support they had there. If you rebel against them, they'll feel even more isolated and unhappy.

Also, you will want to embrace your family's ethnic heritage, and let your parents know you're proud of your ancestry. If they speak a different language and you can communicate well in that language, continue to speak that language to them at home. Participate in your family's traditions and celebrations. Honor your parents by respecting them and the values they value.

Still, you don't have to be an outcast at school. You can find ways to fit into the world you live in now. You may want to dress like your friends and do many of the things your friends do. But try not to needlessly offend your parents. For example, if your parents grew up in a culture where women dress extremely modestly, you probably don't want to go for the Britney Spears look. Stay away from those extreme behaviors that are even bizarre by American standards. Again, talk to your parents, and try to help them understand your world (which is also theirs). Open their eyes with gentleness and respect, and they will be more open to supporting you.

"MY PARENTS ARE BAD EXAMPLES FOR ME"

As I wrote earlier, just because your parents step in a pile of cow manure, it doesn't mean you need to do the same thing. If your parents don't set a good example for you to follow, then don't follow their example. You're smart enough to know the right thing to do, even if they don't.

Parents are human and make mistakes in judgment. Sometimes they develop bad habits that they just can't break. Some parents smoke cigarettes, use foul language, drink too much, use drugs, commit adultery, track mud in the house, spit in the fireplace, and belch in public. They don't set good examples for their kids.

Fortunately, you also have brains and a lot of good sense. Otherwise you wouldn't be reading this book. Take heart. Down through history, a lot of bad examples have been the parents of a lot of good examples. Look at Jesus' family tree in Matthew 1. Some of Jesus' ancestors were murderers, prostitutes, and unsavory characters of all kinds. Despite all those bad examples, Jesus turned out pretty well, don't you think? So can you!

I have tried to improve my attitude, but my mom just keeps on getting angry. Everything I do ticks her off. She yells at me not to do something, but yet she turns around and does it herself, and she just laughs about it when she does it.

—Heidi, age 14

If your parents are involved in things that embarrass you, make you uncomfortable, or are harmful, immoral, unhealthy, or dangerous, you have a right to express your concern and dismay. Talk to them respectfully about these things, and let them know how you feel. You can offer to help them if that's possible. But you can't change your parents unless they're willing to change on their own. And remember—if your parents put you or your siblings at serious risk with their behavior, call someone who can give you some advice. It might be best for you to live with a grandparent or someone else who can provide you with a safe place to live.

Pray for your parents, and follow their example when you know they do the right thing. When you know they aren't, keep praying anyway. You can make the choice now to put yourself in a position where your own children will be proud to follow in your footsteps. It's entirely up to you.

"MY PARENTS ARE ABUSIVE" – – – – – –

If your parent or stepparent abuses you either physically or sexually, you should get help immediately.

Physical abuse can take many forms. Sadly, some parents choose anger over affection, violence over communication. Even parents who love their children deeply can lose control of their tempers and resort to such things as grabbing their kids, shaking them violently, throwing things at them, or hitting them with their hands, fists, or other objects. Why would a parent do this? There may be many reasons, but it's possible that their own parents treated them the same way when they were young.

In the not-too-distant past it was common for parents to take their children out to the woodshed and spank them with a paddle or some other object that would inflict pain as a form of punishment. Some parents would do this with a tear in their eye and say, *"This hurts me more than it hurts you."* Others might do it out of anger or in an attempt to "beat some sense" into their children. If your parents remember this as the way they were brought up, they may feel this is the best way to discipline you.

Is spanking physical abuse? Not everyone thinks so. When parents discipline their children lovingly with a spanking, they often believe they're doing the right thing. They may believe

– – – – – – – – – – – – – – – –

strongly in the proverb that says, "He who spares the rod hates his son, but he who loves him is careful to discipline him" (Proverbs 13:24). They're trying to teach their children that bad behavior is unacceptable and often causes pain.

But when parents lose control and resort to anger and physical violence to deal with their children's misbehavior, they may have a serious problem. If you have a parent who repeatedly hits you or throws things at you, or if you have been injured, cut, or bruised by a parent, this is definitely abuse, and it should be reported to someone who can get help for you and for your parents. Don't resort to physical violence yourself.

Sexual abuse (when an adult touches you inappropriately or attempts to perform a sexual act with you) is a criminal offense, and it is *always* wrong. Get help immediately.

If you believe you have been abused physically or sexually, find a school counselor or teacher, a pastor or youth worker, a police officer, or some other adult you trust to talk to. You can also get help from the National Child Abuse Hotline, which you can call toll-free at 1-800-4-A-CHILD (1-800-422-4453). Don't let embarrassment or fear keep you from doing the right thing. Once you tell someone, you can begin the healing process for both you and your family.

"MY PARENTS DON'T LISTEN TO ME"

If your parents don't listen to you very well, don't take it too personally. Almost all parents have to be retrained to listen to their kids when they become teenagers. When you were little, you probably didn't have much to say that was worth listening to. In a sense, you taught them not to listen to you by jabbering on endlessly about those Saturday morning cartoons or whining about who got the biggest cookie. They did their best to pay attention, but it was no use. Their eyes would simply glaze over, and they would say, "Not now, dear. It's time for your nap."

Now you have to teach them that you do, in fact, have important things to say. And the best way to teach them is to become a good listener yourself. If you listen to them, they'll be so impressed with what a good listener you are they'll want to become better listeners themselves. Go back to Chapter Four, and read the suggestions on how to make listening a F-A-D. When you listen to your parents respectfully, they'll get the message and start listening to you in the same manner.

This may take time, so don't give up. If they seem too busy or too distracted or too impressed with the sound of their own voice, let them know you really do want to talk to them, and you want them to listen to what you have to say. Send them a letter or e-mail if you can't get them to listen to that. You may need to suggest a time or place when you can sit down and have a real conversation. Keep trying, and before long, their ears will be retrained.

"MY PARENTS ARE NOT MY REAL PARENTS" – – – – – – –

If you live in a foster home or with grandparents or an uncle or aunt, or if you're adopted, your parents are not your real parents only by virtue of a technicality. They didn't actually provide the sperm and egg that produced you. But in every other way, they chose to be your parents because they love you and care about you, and you should be grateful. You may be tempted to think you don't need to obey people who are not your real parents, but remember that the command to honor your parents in the Bible doesn't limit itself to birth parents. And neither does anything in this book.

- - - - - "MY PARENTS ARE CHEAP"

So they won't give you the money you want? They won't buy you all the stuff you think everybody your age should have? Your friends get all kinds of perks you don't?

Well, consider yourself lucky. Just for fun, take out a piece of paper, and make a list of all the heroic historical figures you can think of—you know, people like Abraham Lincoln, Martin Luther King, Mother Teresa, and so on. Go ahead, I'll wait...

Got it? Okay, now what do you think these people all have in common? If you haven't figured it out on your own, I'll tell you. Unless you put Bill Gates on your list, it's likely that they all grew up in poverty. What made them great is that they had to overcome all kinds of obstacles in life to achieve their greatness.

Am I suggesting that poverty is a good thing? No. But neither is over-indulgence. You won't find too many heroes who had everything handed to them on a silver platter when they were kids. Over-indulgence only leads to greed, laziness, and unhappiness. You can be thankful if your parents don't give you everything you want.

Parents love to provide all their kids needs, but not all they want. Good parents won't do it even if they can. And in case you didn't know, there is a big difference between needs and wants. It's okay to want things, but you shouldn't expect or require your parents or anyone else to provide them for you.

> *My parents are really stingy about money. They think I can wear clothes from the fifth grade.*
> —Kaitlyn, age 13

For example, my son wanted a new pair of basketball shoes that cost a hundred dollars. He could get perfectly adequate shoes for $40, but he insisted on those expensive shoes. So I gave him $40 (which was all I was willing to spend on shoes), and told him to go buy any pair of shoes he wanted. Suddenly he realized his problem. He *wanted* those expensive shoes, but he *needed* sixty bucks. And since he didn't have sixty bucks, he settled for a good pair of $40 shoes.

Look, if your cheapo parents won't buy you everything you want, maybe you want too much. Ask yourself: can you live without it? Maybe you need to scale down your wish list to something reasonable or figure out some other way to finance it. The best way is to earn it. Don't play the gimme-gimme game with your parents. Nothing in life is free. Just as your folks have to work for a living, so will you. Be grateful for what your parents provide for you now, and figure out how to get everything else you want on your own.

"I CAN'T TELL MY PARENTS WHAT I'VE DONE" - - - - -

You're not alone. Most kids keep secrets from their parents. In fact, there's a good chance your parents did some things as teenagers that their parents don't know about to this day. No law says you have to tell your parents *everything* you've done. You do have a right to *some* privacy in your life.

But if you've done something wrong that concerns you, it might be wise to tell your parents anyway. You can be sure they'll be even more hurt and more upset if they find out from someone else. You'll face tougher consequences and lose even more trust. Remember what we wrote earlier about heading them off at the pass. In most cases you'll be much better off if you tell them yourself before they find out from another source.

> I made a bad mistake by having sex with my boyfriend last year. I made a decision after that to never do it again, but I can't tell my parents about it. I wish I could because I know that God has forgiven me, and I'm proud that I have chosen to stay pure.
> —Kylie, age 16

And your parents may be able to give you the forgiveness, guidance, and support you need. If you experimented with drugs or alcohol, for example, or are sexually active, or committed a crime, you put yourself and others at serious risk. The best thing you can do is admit to yourself and to your parents that you have a problem and allow the people who love you the most to help you. I know a woman who secretly had an abortion as a teenager, which literally destroyed her life. Besides the guilt and depression she suffered for many years, she was never able to marry and have children of her own. If her parents had known about her pregnancy when it happened, they would surely have helped her make a better decision than the one she made.

I know it's hard to disappoint your parents or to face the consequences of your actions, but in most cases confession is the best and fastest route to healing and forgiveness. Your parents love you and want the best for you even when you mess up. If you believe you're responsible enough to make your own decisions, then you should accept the responsibility to own up to your mistakes.

And remember this—God is there for you even when your parents are not. If you can't tell your parents, tell God. He wants to heal you and forgive you, and he will. "If we confess our sins, he is faithful and just and will forgive us our sins and purify us from all unrighteousness" (1 John 1:9). When you know you've been forgiven by your Heavenly Father, it becomes a whole lot easier to face the music with your parents and anyone else you've offended.

"MY PARENTS DON'T WANT ME TO LEAVE HOME"

Parents have many reasons why they don't want their kids to leave home.

Some parents' identities are wrapped up in their roles as parents. This is especially true for mothers who sacrificed pursuing careers to stay home to be full-time moms. When their kids get old enough to leave home, they just have a hard time letting go.

Some parents are afraid for their kids to leave because their marriages are on shaky ground. For years, their children provided the glue that held the family together. When the kids leave, they know they'll have to face the problems in their marriage, and they may not be prepared for that. Sadly, some marriages don't survive the empty nest.

Other parents just feel that their parenting job is never quite over. Perfectionist parents are especially reluctant to let go. They don't think they're finished until they mold their children into the kind of people they want them to be. Of course, they never accomplish this, so they try to keep you at home for as long as they can. Sometimes they'll deliberately make you dependent on them as long as possible so that you can't leave.

Regardless, your goal should be to "leave and cleave" as the Bible puts it (Genesis 2:24) as soon as you're able to live on your own. One easy way to do this is to go away to college, if you have the chance, and live in a dorm. If you stay at home while you attend college, you can expect to be treated much the same way you were treated as a teenager until graduation, with rules and expectations that remain pretty much in place. This is to be expected because your parents do have the right to make and enforce the rules in their house.

Don't leave home before you're ready, of course, but you should prepare yourself for life on your own. Even if you have to live in the same house with your parents after you're old enough to be on your own, you should set some boundaries that will provide you with a healthy separation from Mom and Dad. For example, you should volunteer to cover your own expenses, perhaps even pay rent on your room. Don't be a freeloader. The longer you depend on your parents to pay your way, the longer you give them permission (and the right) to treat you like a child. This will seriously stunt your growth!

If you are certain your parents are having a hard time accepting your eventual departure from home, talk to them about it. Prove to them with your behavior that you have what it takes to survive on your own. Take responsibility for yourself, and let them know you can make good decisions. They won't give you their blessing to leave home until they feel certain they can trust you to be responsible.

If you don't go away to college, consider going on a short-term mission trip that will take you away from home for an extended period of time. This will give both you and your parents a little experience at separation.

"MY PARENTS THINK THEY KNOW EVERYTHING"

Well, they may know a lot about *some* things (like how to diversify an investment portfolio or prepare a tuna casserole), but most parents I know plead total ignorance when it comes to dealing with you. Most parents don't think they know squat.

Not that they'll admit this to you, of course. They would rather not undermine their authority by giving you permission to question or disregard everything they say. They may not know everything, but they aren't THAT stupid.

Here's the deal. When parents feel under attack, they are likely to pretend they know everything as a kind of defense mechanism or even as a counter-offensive to recover some of their lost or eroding power. They have a need to save face, to reestablish their rightful place as parents with authority. Sometimes they just say or do what they remember their own parents saying or doing in similar situations. Desperate people do desperate things.

At times like this parents don't always make a lot of sense. *"Okay, go to that party and see what happens! Go ahead; throw away your future! Don't you know that half the kids who go to parties like this end up as alcoholics or drug addicts? Some never make it home alive! Listen to me! I don't want to have to go down to the morgue tonight to identify your sorry remains! How could you even think of putting us through an ordeal like that?"*

By the way, it's helpful to remember that some questions are best left unanswered. When things heat up like this, it's usually best to let them cool down. One thing's for sure. The more you challenge your parents' authority, the more they'll dig in, and your options become fewer and fewer. Nobody wins in a shouting match.

Parents know a lot more than you want to give them credit for, but believe me, they don't think they know everything. More often than not, that's because you won't give them the information they need. In the absence of information, they are forced to make wild guesses, erroneous assumptions, and do the best they can. You can help them out by being more up -ront and telling them what's going on in your life. The more you tell them, the less they'll need to pretend they know what they don't.

"MY PARENTS ARE EMBARRASSING TO ME" - - - - - - - -

Have one of your parents ever...
- Had a credit card refused while shopping with you?
- Visited you at your job and announced to all the other customers that you're her child?
- Picked you up from school with curlers in her hair?
- Picked you up from school in his work truck?
- And then honked the horn?
- Tried to tell a joke to your friends but forgot the punch line?
- Taken pictures of you and your date before you left home?
- Hugged you right after you won the swim meet?
- Run out of gas while driving you and your friends to the mall?
- Asked your new friend how his parents voted in the last election?
- Turned your underwear pink by washing them with your sister's red sweatshirt?

Yeah, parents can be pretty embarrassing at times. But don't be too hard on them. They're just adults who don't remember how they were embarrassed by their own parents. Besides, they think they're pretty far out by their own standards, even if they are so, well, 20 years ago. You can't change them, really, and it's doubtful you'd want to anyway. After all, you probably don't want parents who wear the same clothes, listen to the same kind of music, and do the same things you do. That would be even more embarrassing.

So don't worry too much about being embarrassed by your mom and dad. Parents are *supposed* to be embarrassing. Invite them into your world, and you may be surprised that your friends aren't as embarrassed by them as you are. They may even think your parents are pretty cool.

If your parents are physically handicapped, or speak with an accent, or a weight problem, or are different in some other way, remember that they need your love and acceptance even more. Don't be embarrassed or ashamed of them. You'll actually look a lot worse in the eyes of others if you are. Read the powerful story in the sidebar that teaches an important lesson about acceptance

A soldier was finally coming home after having fought in the war. He called his parents from San Francisco.

"Mom and Dad, I'm coming home, but I've a favor to ask. I have a friend I'd like to bring home with me."

"Sure," they replied. "We'd love to meet him."

"There's something you should know," the son continued. "He was hurt pretty badly in the fighting. He stepped on a land mine and lost an arm and a leg. He has nowhere else to go, and I want him to come live with us."

"I'm sorry to hear that, son. Maybe we can help him find somewhere to live."

"No, Mom and Dad, I want him to live with us."

"Son," said the father, "you don't know what you're asking. Someone with such a handicap would be a terrible burden to us. We have our own lives to live, and we can't let something like this interfere with our lives. I think you should just come on home and forget about this guy. He'll find a way to live on his own."

At that point, the son hung up the phone. The parents heard nothing more from him. A few days later, however, they received a call from the San Francisco police. Their son died after falling from a building, they were told. The police believed it was suicide.

The grief-stricken parents flew to San Francisco and were taken to the city morgue to identify the body of their son. They recognized him, but to their horror they also discovered something they didn't know—their son had only one arm and one leg.

"Accept one another, then, just as Christ accepted you, in order to bring praise to God." (Romans 15:7)

CLIFFS NOTES

(IN CASE YOU NEED TO GET UNGROUNDED QUICKLY)

If you're starting with this chapter, no problem. But I hope you'll go back and read the rest of the book too. It's really not all that boring and it has some pretty cool cartoons, in case you like to just look at the pictures.

But for your convenience, here's a quick summary of this masterpiece of literature in case you need to convince your parents you actually read it instead of wasting your time playing Galaxy Wars on your computer.

You're welcome!

CHAPTER ONE

This chapter contains a bunch of really weird myths about parents. They may sound true, BUT THEY'RE NOT.

Here's an example. *When Parents Ask You To Do Chores, They Actually Expect You To Do Them.* See what I mean? That's a myth! But you probably knew that already. So let's go on to chapter two.

CHAPTER TWO

This is just the opposite of Chapter One. It contains facts about your parents that you can take to the bank. They may sound false, but THEY ARE ABSOLUTELY TRUE, and you need to remember them.

Here's an example. "PARENTS HAVE LOTS OF MONEY, AND THEY WANT TO GIVE IT ALL TO YOU." Some kids don't realize this, so they never ask. Now you know.

CHAPTER THREE

This chapter gives you a list of THINGS YOU NEVER WANT TO DO at home. If you blow it and do these things, you'll really get yourself in hot water.

Here's an example. "ALWAYS BE NICE TO YOUR SISTER." Are you kidding? Be nice to your sister and see what happens. Your parents will know for sure that you're up to no good.

CHAPTER FOUR

This is another just-the-opposite chapter. This chapter is a list of THINGS YOU DEFINITELY WANT TO DO at home. Give them a try and you'll score all kinds of points with mom and dad.

For example, "TELL YOUR MOM SHE NEEDS TO GO ON A DIET." She has probably been waiting for someone to remind her she's been getting a little chunky lately, so why not be the first. She'll be so glad you are concerned about her appearance.

CHAPTER FIVE

This chapter is for kids who have special parent problems, like "MY PARENTS ARE ZOMBIES" or "MY MOM CAN BEAT ME ONE-ON-ONE IN HOOPS." My advice to teenagers with serious problems like these is simply: deal with it.

CHAPTER SIX

Um, you're in chapter six right now, so figure it out for yourself.

Well, there you go. The whole book in a nutshell. But maybe you still need to go back and read it for yourself. If you only read the Cliffs Notes, you might get something wrong, and I can't be held responsible for that.

Your friend and author,
Wayne Rice